Gnome Sneezes

 Written by: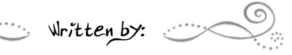

Faye Folkie

Illustrated by:

Faye Folkie and Ogre G. Stamps

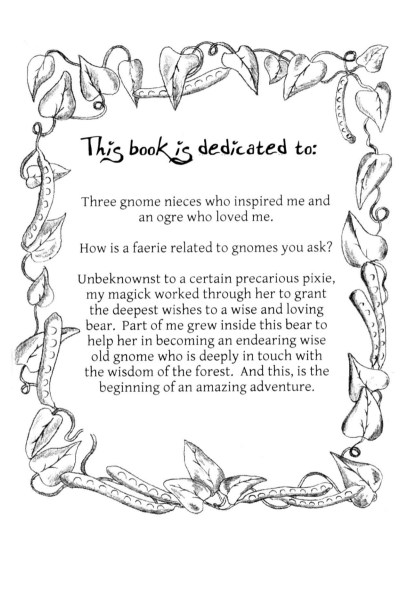

This book is dedicated to:

Three gnome nieces who inspired me and
an ogre who loved me.

How is a faerie related to gnomes you ask?

Unbeknownst to a certain precarious pixie,
my magick worked through her to grant
the deepest wishes to a wise and loving
bear. Part of me grew inside this bear to
help her in becoming an endearing wise
old gnome who is deeply in touch with
the wisdom of the forest. And this, is the
beginning of an amazing adventure.

Table of Contents

CHAPTER 1

Peptiflitter

"Now focus Alexh. You must be light as a feather. Povh shouldn't be feelin your weight against him." Papa continued to give direction as the little gnome haphazardly glided through the trees on the back of her glider.

Leaves and twigs brushed past her face as they glided between the gusts of wind. Alexh was trying to ignore the rise and fall of her stomach as she trailed far behind her sisters who rode faster and more gracefully. She felt positive that the giggling ahead was directly aimed at her. Somehow she hadn't lucked into a current with the right lift. Perhaps her gliders tail was too short or too long. Maybe her sisters just had an unfair advantage due to being thinner and lighter.

Alexh glared at her sisters as they joyfully rode each draft like they were weightless leaves furling, twirling and swooping between the trees. They were in the moment and had completely forgotten about Alexh bobbing and drifting awkwardly behind them. Just as the perfect blast of air lifted Alexh higher than her sisters, the most obtrusive mess of gnarly vines got in her way.

Alexh tugged harder on Povh's fur attempting to gain more control of the ride. This was a little uncomfortable for Povh, but he tried as hard as he could to please Alexh. They began to roam higher and faster than her sisters, until something brought their ride to a painful halt in mid-air. Alexh and her glider had drifted right into a knotted bundle of hanging vines.

"Alexh, there is a way out just behind Povh!" shouted Megan.

"I know how to get out!" As often as I get stuck in these things she thought to herself.

1

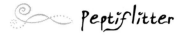

Papa tried to give her guidance, "Let Povh lead ya out. Let go a them vines!"

Alexh continued to pull on the vines anyway, causing them to become tighter and tighter.

Povh squealed because he couldn't stand feeling trapped. He quickly chewed on the vines tightening around him and climbed out, leaving Alexh still hanging.

Megan and Sam began to laugh, making Alexh very angry. The little gnome gave one last tug, as the chewed ends slipped away. Alexh was released from the vines but landed very hard on the branch below her.

Papa began to lightly scold her for not listening, "Alexh, yer not learnin cause yer not listenin. You should be mind'n me and you should be listenin to Povh."

"That's silly. Povh can't talk."

"Listen wit yer heart. You need to be in the moment wit him. He knows more than you realize...."

Mama cut him short, "Oh Papa, let them go pick berries. It's their birthday. No need to study so hard today. You girls go collect the best berries you can find, and hurry back, now."

As the girls took off Papa scoffed at Mama, "She's so far behind on her studies you know. She should be gliding better, healing animals and learning to make fine..."

Gnome Sneezes

Mama put her finger over his lips, "I'll hear no more out of you. Get me the honey for the cakes and right away wit yeh."

Papa opened his mouth, as if to have an argument, but then just gave his very best "Hmf!" The only thing he could think of as Mama had hurried back into the underground.
The girls raced on their gliders toward the lake next to their favorite berry bush. Alexh really wanted to get there first but she glided right into another bundle of vines. She got completely tangled, while her sisters made it to the lake first. Alexh was very upset. She yelled at Povh, "Stop landing in the vines!" Then she sneezed. The vines seemed to tighten around her and then she noticed they were covered in green beans. "Augh, I hate green beans! "Ishu, ishu" she sneezed. Then squirrels began to throw nuts at her. "I hate squirrels! Ishu!" These squirrels had become particularly good at locating Alexh and beaming her with nuts, right on the noggin.

By the time she and Povh became free of the vine and made it to the lake, Megan and Sam were playing in the water with their gliders. Alexh yelled, "You can't swim! We're supposed to get berries! Get out NOW!"

The two playful gnomes began to chant, "Nah nah you can't tell us what to do."

Alexh threw a rock at them, lost balance and fell into the water. She landed right on top of a sleeping turtle, who nipped her toe. She squealed and jumped back out of the water. "Why does everything in this forest hate me? I hate this forest!" She ran behind the bush and cried. Povh tried to comfort her by offering a big juicy bug, but she was in no mood to be comforted. "Leave me alone. I don't eat bugs!"

The other two gnomes waited for Alexh to calm down before climbing out of the water. Alexh was careful to only gather berries. The last time they went to gather berries, Alexh had also gathered seeds and small nuts. She found later that the "seeds" were mostly squirrel poop, which explained the stains on her hands, cloths and the inside of her pack. She smelled terrible. No one meant to make her feel bad, but it was hard not to laugh. She vowed to never gather seeds again.

Mama and Papa greeted them with three tasty acorn birthday cakes. Their names were carefully drizzled over the top with a honey blueberry drizzle. The girls eyed the sweet cakes that were their very favorite snack.

Papa announced, "And we'll be going to dinner in the gnome village tomorrow!" Megan and Sam exclaimed, "Yay!" Alexh exclaimed, "No, I hate going to the village!"
This wasn't entirely true, however. She really longed for the interaction with other gnomes her age, but something generally went wrong on these trips. Something large would accidentally sit on her or try to eat her. Somehow she always ended up wet or dirty or somehow humiliated. Papa understood her feelings, but felt that an incident free visit was just around the corner. He put his arms around her, "Oh Alexh, it'll be okay this time. I'll be lookin out for yeh."

Just then, a pixie flew up the gnome tunnel and all through the kitchen. She made herself really small to tease and have fun with the three girls on their birthday. The underground home was wild with the excitement of chasing, yelling and laughing. Alexh's birthday cake was knocked right out of

Mama's hands and broke into a million pieces. The pixie dashed out of sight and Alexh again yelled, "The forest hates me! I hate everyone!"

and ran crying to bed. Her sisters wanted to share with her, but Alexh just wanted this to be the end of another very bad day.

Mama tucked her in. Alexh cried, "Mama, why does all the bad stuff happen to me? This is the third birthday in a row that only my cake gets ruined. Why does the forest hate me?" Mama snuggled up and whispered, "Oh Alexh, the forest doesn't hate you. Why would the forest not be loven a little freckle face like you?" wiping her tears away. "The forest is big and grand. It's beyond anything we'll even know. There's no reason to be single'n out one tiny little gnome like you. The forest loves everyone. Sometimes when we play a lil' rough its only knowin is to play rough right back."

Alexh bolted up, "That makes no sense! I didn't do anything to make it so rough. The forest is just mean!" Then she buried her head under the covers and cried.

"Let her cry it out Mama." said Papa. "It will just take her time to find her peace. She'll be fine." Mama,

Papa and the two gnomes delighted on acorn cakes and story time by candle light. Papa told stories about nasty goblins, rotten pixies and other scary things that creep into their part of the forest. He said they sneak in quietly from another world. They are silent as they slither, crawl, fly and climb in through their secret ways. You may never see these sneaky creatures due to their ability to disguise themselves with the magick of another world and ways that are not agreeable to gnomes. Then Papa reminded the girls, "These other faerie folk are not like gnomes; not like gnomes at all."

5

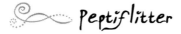 Peptiflitter

Alexh's crying and sneezing had finally transformed into
snoring. Mama tucked the other two gnomes carefully into bed
with her. Papa put the gliders out for night watch and joined
Mama for a good night sleep.
A storm had blown over their oak tree throughout evening.
The thunder and wind had died down to a gentle rumbling
for the rest of the night. Their oak had mysteriously sprouted
green beans, which completely covered the outside of their
home. Strange things were beginning to happen.

Papa held Mama, "Oh Mama, there are more green beans than
ever out there. They've even started growing from the tree
itself."

"Ah, so it's gettin worse. I don't know why she hates the darn
green beans so much."

"Perhaps because you cook them so much?"

"I only cook them because there are so many!"

"No matter Mama. If it weren't green beans it would be
something else sprouting all over."

"We will have to tell her tomorrow."

"I was hopin this would all pass. Perhaps this is a Mama
daughter thing?" Papa said, staring at his toes.

"No. We'll be doin this together. She needs to know we are
all here to support her. There will be no riskin it gettin any
worse."

"Agreed Mama. We'll have a nice chit-chat over breakfast."
He said as he rubbed his round firm tummy.

That night Alexh dreamt she found a lucky stone. She carried

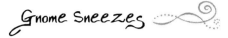

it around in the pocket of her sweater. Nothing bothered her, nothing fell on her and she never fell into anything. She glided happily through the trees and enjoyed the forest. Povh was especially graceful as he glided up rather than down. Soon she was gliding far above the trees and could see that the forest stretched on forever.

Thud! Alexh's sisters accidentally pushed her out of bed.

"Grrrrr" she mumbled and headed into the next room where Mama had berries and granola waiting for them. Megan and Sam scrambled behind her to get to breakfast before their gliders wake from their morning nap. The two sisters were cooing and enjoying sweet berries but Alexh somehow got all sour ones.

Alexh threw down the sour berries and cried, "This isn't fair!" Then she ran out of the hollow and jumped onto Povh, who was sound asleep just outside. Povh was very startled and jumped up into the tree and began springing from branch to branch. Alexh was so angry she could not stop the momentum for a very long time. All the way Alexh cried and even sneezed, "Ishu, ishu!". Green beans sprouted on some of the trees as they passed. Alexh never noticed. Some of those green beans hatched furry purple spiders with large red eyes. Alexh never knew.

By the time she was calm again, she realized she didn't know quite where she had ended up. "I wonder how far we've gone. Maybe this is where I find my lucky stone. Then all the bad luck will go away forever. If I have good luck, it will be easier to find our way home Povh." So, Alexh began looking under everything for a stone that looked just like the one in her dream. She looked inside trees, which sometimes got her into trouble, when they were already occupied. Alexh had been growled at, nipped, chased and pelted with nuts. Everywhere she looked she only found a very angry animal who didn't'

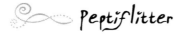

appreciate being disturbed.

It began to get late when Alexh climbed onto a large mushroom and heard faint giggling. She looked up and saw the culprit high in a flowering tree. A little pixie had been watching her the whole time. Alexh yelled, "What's so funny?!"

"You. You're always peptiflitter!" as she zipped down to Alexh.

"Hey! You're the same pixie who ruined my cake!" Alexh was still very cross with her.

The pixie turned her head up and away with an arrogant tone piped, "I didn't ruin your cake. It would have been just fine if you weren't so peptiflitter all the time."

"What's that?"

The playful little pixie crept closer and told her, "That's when you're all eaten up with anger all the time. You don't even know how to not be eaten by the angry bug anymore. It's so funny to watch." And then she giggled at Alexh.

"It's NOT funny!" Alexh puffed as a mushy spoiled fruit fell right on her head.

"Hahahaha! Yes it is. It makes stuff happen to you all the time. You are so funny!

"Being pepi, pepti, pepti-whatsit makes my bad luck?"

"Peptiflitter. It's a pixie word. Yeppers you're the biggest fun in the whole forest."

"But I don't want bad luck. How do I get rid of it?"

"Oh, you can't. Every bit of your body is used to being peptiflitter. It's too hard to stop. You'd have to get you're body unused to it'.
Alexh looked down at her little body and wondered where to place the blame.

The expressive little pixie rolled her eyes, shook her head and continued, "You silly gnome. You're way too young to understand complicated pixie stuff. You have a little brain that makes pepti's." She held her hands up forming a shape much like a tiny nut and continued. "When you're mad the pepti's rush into your body and give you the flitters. It feels like a bolt of energy and reacts with every single chemical in your body in some way. Before it's done playing tricks in there it'll totally mess up your whole bodies magnetism."

The pixie began to run around in circles waving her arms looking crazy. "Then all kinds of bad stuff gets magnetized to you!" and then she pounced on Alexh liked a crazed kitten and tickled her all over.

Alexh screamed and scurried away. Panting, she peaked out from behind another large mushroom, "What about pixies? Do pixies get peptiflitter?"
"Heck no." (looking a bit full of herself) "We just think happy thoughts and can see how funny everything is."

"Then teach me how to do that!"

"Hmmmm" she thought about it. Then a mischievous smile appeared upon her otherwise sweet face. "Okay, but everything I do has to be funny to you. You have to laugh and you have to do whatever I say."

Alexh, looking worried, "I think I'm going to regret this."

"You want to loose the bad luck right?"

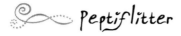 *Peptiflitter*

"Yeah"

"Coolios! It's a deal. My name is Minx and I'm your teacher."

Alexh slowly stepped closer to Minx, "But how do you laugh at everything Minx? Don't you have to take some things seriously?"

"You just have to learn to see the humor in the forest. We pixies know how to take it easy. It's easy. Sparkle Magic! I can't wait to tell the faeries about you and Sky Kitty here. You're my new project. Can't wait to see the look on those faeries faces when, me, a pixie helps out an ordinary woods gnome like you. Ha! I'll show them how smart I am." Just then, another pixie from above tipped a large tree flower full of water so that it landed right on Minx.

Alexh began to laugh and point.

Minx smirked at Alexh, "Oh, you think that's funny? Lesson number one; laugh at yourself." She darted straight up through the branches of the flowering tree, hitting all the tree flowers she could and dumping lots of water right onto Alexh.

"Augh! Now I'm cold and wet!" Minx dashed straight back down, still sopping wet, mouth puckered, cheeks blown up and with her tiny finger pointing at Alexh. Alexh thought she looked ridiculous and started laughing again.

"Coolios! This is going to be easy. Now if you can just keep this up for the next twenty one days…"

"Twenty one days! I have to go home."

"You can't go home. You're my project. Besides, you don't know you're way home and I'm not going all the way back right now."

Gnome Sneezes

Alexh began to whine, "But I'll be in trouble."
Minx shrugged one shoulder, "Not for twenty one days."
Alexh puckered her lower lip and began to sniffle.

"Don't get all weepy eyed on me freckle face. We want to cure you, right?"
"Yeah"

"Well, there's no other way." Minx smiled with her hands in the air. "And… Silly Bean, it's getting late. It's time for lesson two. You wait here." Then she dashed away.

Alexh rode Povh up the tree and filled a big cavern with fallen tree flowers. This made a cushy nest for the evening. "Hmm. I guess she means well, Povh. I sure do miss my Mama and Papa though.

She looked up at the darkening sky, "Hey forest, tell my family that I miss them. Tell them I'm okay and I'm not mad anymore. I'm going to be all better when I get back. I'll be the luckiest gnome in the whole forest." Then she closed her eyes, smiled and remembered how great her family has always been. While her eyes were still closed a little elemental glowed bright. He remembered where the gnomes lived and carried the message away.

Minx reappeared with warm acorn bread.

"Wow Minx, where did you get it?"

"Oh the tree elves sometimes leave them out to cool. I thought you'd like it."

The two relaxed in the flowers and enjoyed the freshly baked bread.

"What's lesson two?"

11

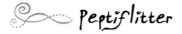 Peptiflitter

"Just kickin it. You gotta get really good at this because tomorrow we're gonna pixie spy all day."

"That sounds easy."

"Yeppers, and all ya gotta do is keep on smiling and keep the fur-ball quiet." Minx yawned as Povh chattered at her. "You're a lot nicer when you're sleepy Minx."

"Ha! Lucky for you."

"Here Povh, have some acorn bread." Minx began to size up the funny little creature that seemed to be very protective of Alexh. "You are very close to your pet, aren't you."

"Yeah, he's pretty great except he's probably the clumsiest glider in all of gnome history."

"Awe, don't blame Povh, it's just communication. It'll get better Silly Head."

Then they cuddled up with Povh snuggled within the deep pile of tree flowers and fell fast to sleep.

On the other end of the forest, Papa just received the elemental message. "Mama! It's those darn pixies again! Always stealing something, they are. Now they've got our Alexh!"

"Oh Papa. Don't you go runnin off. The forest'll be watchin' our baby. You need to trust the forest now. It's time she knew herself."

"I'll not be trustin those darn pixies! Always meddlin with something they autn't!"

"She's become more dangerous to herself these days. Growing closer everyday to where you were the day I met yeh. The

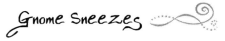

forest has intervened. Give her a bit of time Papa. She'll return to us soon."

Then Mama turned to the tiny elemental, "You'll be watchin over her, won't yeh?"

The elemental played a pleasant tone that Mama knew meant yes.

"Then off with yeh. Keep us informed."

The tiny bit of light swirled and whirled as it faded into the night.

CHAPTER 2

Differences

Minx started their day by tickling Alexh. Alexh screamed, "Hahahaha! No! I'm going to pee my pants!" But Minx kept right on tickling her until she believed Alexh just might do it. "Good job! Just keep smiling all day Silly Bean and this will be a cinch."

Alexh said, in an exhausted breath, "Being happy sure is tiring." As she headed into the tall grass for a moment of "morning privacy".

"Not once you get used to it! That's what you're going to learn with me. We're going to pixie spy!"

Alexh was trying to avoid getting her heinie bit by a big mean ant as she heard Minx yell out, "Oh yeah, be careful of the

ants back there. If they get your heinie, you won't be able to sit for week!"

"Oh, great." She muttered as she quickly peed and ran back out of the grass with a terrible scowl on her face.

"Did you get bit?"

"No."

"See your luck is changing already. I totally expected one of those buggers to get you."

Alexh looked terribly offended as she seated herself next to a few pieces of stale cake from the night before. "What's this stupid pixie spying? Is that what you were doing on me yesterday?"

"Yeppers, I guess that makes you honorary pixie for a day. Minx started their day by tickling Alexh. Alexh screamed, "Hahahaha! No! I'm going to pee my pants!" But Minx kept right on tickling her until she believed Alexh just might do it. "Good job! Just keep smiling all day Silly Bean and this will be a cinch."

Alexh said, in an exhausted breath, "Being happy sure is tiring." As she headed into the tall grass for a moment of "morning privacy".

"Not once you get used to it! That's what you're going to learn with me. We're going to pixie spy!"

Alexh was trying to avoid getting her heinie bit by a big mean ant as she heard Minx yell out, "Oh yeah, be careful of the ants back there. If they get your heinie, you won't be able to sit for week!"

"Oh, great." She muttered as she quickly peed and ran back out of the grass with a terrible scowl on her face.

"Did you get bit?"

"No."

"See your luck is changing already. I totally expected one of

15

those buggers to get you."

Alexh looked terribly offended as she seated herself next to a few pieces of stale cake from the night before. "What's this stupid pixie spying? Is that what you were doing on me yesterday?"

"Yeppers, I guess that makes you honorary pixie for a day. Try to keep up, because we're going to the other side of that mountain." Minx pointed into the distance, then flittered ahead of Alexh.

"Wait!" Alexh yelled as she tucked the dried cake into her socks because her sweater and pack was left at home. She and Povh bounced and glided through the trees as fast as gnomely possible. She did all she could to keep up and keep smiling, though her smile just made her look constipated. She was very busy worrying about what could possibly go wrong next. Minx flew a few circles around her and Povh, just to tease her about her slowness. "No frowning aloud Dingy Dong!"

"What? I'm smiling. Can't she tell a smile from a frown? You can tell, can't you Povh." Povh made a tiny squeak, as he usually did to respond to Alexh. She felt that was all the affirmation she needed.

Once they landed Minx threw pixie sparkles over the three of them. "They won't be able to see us now Freckle Face. They're not the kind of faerie folk we want to see you and the sky kitty. If the fachan gets too close to you, he could scare you to death!" Minx threw her hands up trying to look scary for Alexh. "Yeppers, all you have to do all day is enjoy the game. Let go of all your worries and everything you thought you knew before, because the rules are all different here."

Alexh looked around and saw lots of strange beings running through a patch of trees surrounded by tall grass and weird plants she had never seen in her part of the forest. The playing field had a boundary of rocks that players may not pass. The creatures were all playing a game that resembled a brutal game of hide and seek.

"They look a little scary to me. Where did they come from? Did they come from the other world that Papa talks about?"

"Yeppers, these faerie folk have come from far away to play Faerie Scout today. Like I said, they can't see us so don't worry. You're not supposed to do that, remember."

Alexh did not like the cocky expressions Minx liked to flash at her. It would be easier to not worry if she didn't keep brining it up, she thought to herself as she made herself comfortable in a low hanging branch with leaves and old bird nesting. "Do you want to cuddle with me?" she asked Povh, but then noticed he had already curled up in another nook and was sound asleep. "Hmf. His snoring would have been distracting anyway."

On each team there were twelve hiders and one scout, who each peeked when counting. This really gave no advantage to any team because the hiders were using magick to disguise what they were doing anyway.

Alexh gasped, "They can't do that! They're cheating."

"Shhhhh. Just watch. We all have unique magick and learn to play the games differently according to our talents. All beings need to learn how their magick is different. You can't expect everybody to play by your rules because we're all totally different. Kinda like there is always more than one way to drown a goblin1.

"To what?"

 # Differences

"It's a pixie saying. Sometimes, it's just fun to drown goblins[1]."

"Why?"

"The point is, Gnomie, when you learn to just sit back and let go of control and your expectations of how things should be, you learn more. Every folkie expresses magickally different and it is respected. You can't expect to control those differences in other folkies. It's a totally different game here. While you're busy focusing on how some other folkie should be, you're not focusing on your own magick.

The Fachan is a perfect example of how trying to take control of anything outside of you makes you lose control of your focus and your magick. He doesn't think; he only reacts. He is the strongest on the field, but has never learned much magick because he wants control over what's around him. It is the magick in your heart that creates all of the possibilities. But losing your temper causes everything around you to just go haywire.

If your mind is free of expectations of others, you get a clear picture of the possibilities. You let go of the expectations and focus on excelling in your magick. Your heart needs this kind of nourishment. The magick comes from the heart and it can create beyond your expectations and imagination.

"My Papa says our kind of magick comes from the forest."

"Yeppers, that's what the gnomes say. Faerie folk are all different like that. Through the heart, from the heart, from the first faeries or from the forest itself, it's all the same."

"It doesn't sound the same. Which way is best?"

---

1   Goblins are not really harmed in this activity. See Glossary.
..

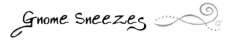

"Are you afraid that the magick won't work?"

"No, just want to know which way is most magickal."

"Silly Bean, magick just is. It doesn't care how you let it work. It isn't how special your way is, it's your belief in magick that makes it work. It is a part of you and everything else. So yes, it's in your heart, my heart and the heart of the forest. You see, it doesn't matter because we're all connected. Focusing on the greater good strengthens the connection"

"But how do I become magickal like you? You're so different from the gnomes."

"All magick gets better when you listen to your heart. See the Fir Darrig?

Alexh looked at the old hunched creatures in red coats and funny hats. Their faces had layers of wrinkles around beady little eyes and a large gaping mouths. How could an entire species be so old? Why would they even consider playing a role in this game? They didn't appear to be in shape for any kind of sport and looked out of place on the field. "Yeah, I see them, but why are they there?"

Minx seemed happy to explain, "Well, they are very old beings and are still slow to learn to let go of control of everything outside of them.

19

# Differences

Their temperament has held them back. They still demand control over everything around them and therefore they too pay less attention to their heart and their personal growth. They have the magick to create nothing more than illusion." Minx pointed to the action on the field, "Watch, every time a Fir Darrig gets aggravated on the field, a Fachan just slaps them in the head with the mace! Now that Fir Darrig has disappeared into their world and you have one less Fir Darrig on the field. Meanwhile, the Ghillie Dhu are safely moving across the field unseen. They have not participated in the struggle at all."

Alexh watched these three very different and peculiar types of beings. Fir Darrigs changed into a variety of creatures as the fachans chased them about the field. Their forms often tricked the scout fachan into hitting one of their own. "What do you mean, they haven't participated? Aren't they in the game? It doesn't look like they are in the game."

"Gillie dhu are not particularly strong. They will not win this game through force. Anytime you are using force to gain something, you have committed yourself to the struggle. If you feel that you are struggling to get something done, it is because you are not using your talents. You have to consider your magick whenever you find yourself trying to do something that does not come easily. Does that happen to you?"

"I don't have any magick."

Minx pointed her finger at Alexh while cocking her had back and forth she poignantly said, "You, are wrong."

Alexh furrowed her brow at Minx, crossed her arms and then focused on the game. Each faerie type is represented in the scouts. The object of the game is for the scouts to tag the opponents with iron. Faerie folkies cannot do magick once they've been tagged with iron. Once tagged, they quickly disappear to the land they came from in order to heal from

20

iron poisoning.

The Fachans had only one arm, one leg, one eye, one nose, and one very large mouth. They possessed very little magickal power. Their only magick was the ability to hide in one place, but then show up somewhere else. It did them little good because they're so awkward, noisy and clumsy. Their bodies were covered in black fur with bright blue feathers around the neck. Each Fachan carried a large club joined to a rounded metal ball by a chain. These Fachans were very strong and quick to swing their weapon at anything that moved. The Fachan scout could hop great distances with ease and took frequent advantage of their ability to appear and disappear all over the playing field. However, due to their clumsy nature, they often accidentally hit themselves or their own team mates with the iron tipped weapon, knocking them out of the game.

The Fir Darrigs carried a long walking stick that normally is topped with a strange skull. For the purpose of the game it was replaced with a lump of iron. This weapon was very difficult for their scout to swing at opponents. They have little strength and little speed. Even as the scout attempted to look like a larger stronger folkie on the field, they cannot out maneuver nor out frighten the fachan who is champion of terror in the forest. Though the action of the game is clearly in the hand of the fachan, Fir Darrigs are known to be very tricky and can play a good joke on the wisest of forest creatures. They were bound to have other tricks up their little red sleeves.

21

 ## Differences

The Ghillie Dhu did not look much like faerie folk at all.
Before they ran to hide they looked like piles of leaves shaped
into little people. Stretched all over the field, they were too
difficult to see at all. They looked too much like the vines and
leaves already covering the game area. These clever little guys
held mostly still, avoiding the competition and struggle. The
Ghillie Dhu scout made his iron ball very tiny on the end of a
little stick that blended very well with all of the vines covering
the ground. It seemed they made no effort to tag the other
teams at all.

Alexh laughed every time she saw the Fachan scout swing his
mace back and accidentally hit his own team mate on the head.
The Ghillie Dhu must love seeing how clumsy the fachans
are too; because they often tripped Fachans with their tricky
vines. They also tripped the Fir Darrig making it easier for the
Fachan scout to tag them.

As the teams began to dwindle the game began to get more
interesting. There were only four Fachan and three Fir Darrig

22

left on the field. No one could tell how many Ghillie Dhu were left because their spindly little bodies were too difficult to see at all. Also, their whispers ride on the wind, so you can't tell where their voices come from. The Fir Darrigs were getting tired of being knocked around by the big strong Fachans. They finally decided to change their strategy.

As the Fachan scout swung his mace from side to side, thrashing at trees and anything that moved, he noticed something appetizing at the base of a tree. There was a bowl of honey milk and bread with sweet butter sitting unguarded. The Fachan scout raced up to the food and leaned over to lap up a bit of milk when he realized he just kissed an iron ball! The Fir Darrig had created a distraction that the Fachan could not resist. They know that their best chance at causing the Fachans to lose their focus is to distract them any way possible. This is not a difficult task, as the fachan is not very bright either.

Another Fachan grabbed the mace, taking the position of the scout and swung it at the food until the food disappeared and the Fir Darrig that was standing invisible next to the food had also been tagged and sent back home.

Another Fir Darrig then hid bits of iron around the field that held a spell of illusion, making them look like sparkly gems and precious stones. Two of the Fachans grabbed stones before they realized that the stones were really iron. Also, the ground got a little less viney. That could mean that some of the Ghillie Dhu took the bait as well. This distraction proved to be more successful than any other. Fir Darrig have become very knowledgeable of the perfect distraction for all beings and know how to use this to deter them from their focus.

The Fir Darrig, with only two team members left, may be in the lead. The very last Fachan spotted one Fir Darrig disguised as a big fat frog peeking out from under a leaf. He

chased that Fir Darrig around the field swinging his mace, as the Fir Darrig continued to change into a monkey, tarsier, booghopper, ticklebird, goblin, and on and on. But the Fachan did not take his one big eye off this Fir Darrig. In one mighty swing he finally squished the Fir Darrig as a bumble bee. The mace bounced off of the tree, and back at the Fachan, knocking him on the head, and out of the game.

The game came down to only one Fir Darrig, who knew that he was surrounded by tricky Ghillie Dhu. He was trying to be careful not to step on leaves and vines that might be the Ghillie Dhu scout and the hidden iron ball. He knew they were out there, because he could hear them giggling at him. Their giggles rode on the wind and this Fir Darrig's large pointed ears were very sensitive to giggles riding on the wind. It caused the tips to quiver a bit.

The Ghillie Dhu told the other vines to begin moving about. Leaves in the trees began to hear the command of the Ghillie Dhu. The Fir Darrig began smacking everything that moved. It seemed as though the Ghille Dhu must be everywhere, because everything was moving. He panicked, and started running all over the field smacking everything, until he finally stepped right onto the iron ball that was left sitting in plain view. He was just getting too peptiflitter to see what he was doing and the Ghillie Dhu won the game!

Minx jumped up and down, and cheered, "Yay, Ghillie Dhu!"

Alexh looked a bit glum.

"Hey there Frowny Face, what's got you down?"

"I was rooting for the Fachan, cause they're funny."

"Yeah, I guess that's why I root for you Silly Bean. But you want to be more like the Ghillie Dhu if you want to get better

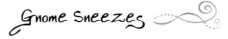

at your riding and lose the bad luck and get good at whatever magick you choose. You're luck won't improve if you don't start letting the fight go."

"Well, I still don't know how to be more like the Ghillie Dhu. I could barely see them!"

Minx began to play with Alexh's long sleek hair, "I know what they look like, and we can fix you right up!"
"Augh, let go."

"I'm going to give you crazy Ghillie Dhu hair. We'll make it black and put lots of weird leaves and mossy clumps, and…."

"No, I like my hair the way it is." Alexh pulled away.

The two teased and played till dark. Neither of them knew that the pixie dust had worn off just as the game had ended. One young Ghillie Dhu noticed them. He found Minx particularly spunky and entertaining. He heard stories about her and always wanted to know what she was really like. He enjoyed listening to the two argue and then he played with Povh after they had gone to sleep. This little Ghillie Dhu was itching for an adventure. None of his folk had noticed that he had slipped away, so he decided he'd tag along behind this peculiar little group for a few days.

CHAPTER 3

Magick

Alexh woke up giggling because Povh was licking her feet. Tickling soon turned to wrestling which could go on for hours between these two, if uninterrupted.

"Hey Freckle-face, today you're going to learn about how controlling your temper and learning yourself from the inside will be the key to opening your magick up to you. There is a whole world of magick and sillisense inside of you to explore once you stop trying to control everything outside of you. Do you know why the Ghillie Dhu won?"

Alexh stood up and stopped laughing to think about the question. "Because no one can see them?"

"Why couldn't the other two teams see them?"

Alexh rolled under some leaves and popped up looking a little like a Ghillie Dhu saying, "Because the Ghillie Dhu were in a clever disguise!"

"Snap dragons and Troll Snot! It's cause they were clever enough to let the other two teams control the game. Those peptiflitter snot-mongers couldn't see that they were knocking each other out of the game! The Fachans and the Fir Darrig were part of the struggle, so they couldn't see the Ghillie Dhu who were not in the struggle with them. Sometimes you have to let go of the control over everything around you in order to learn your lessons and to keep safe. When you do that you also let others learn from their own actions. You're actions interfere with their lessons. Crystal clear miss bossy-pants?" she snapped at Alexh.

"When am I bossy?"

"Only every time you expect your sisters to do things your way." Minx lightly poked Alexh's little nose. "You're journey gets so much easier when you figure out it's no fun trying to be the boss. You can't pay enough attention to your own journey and your own magick when you're focused on everybody else."

Alexh remembered how much work it had been trying to get her sisters to follow her lead. Every time she created an order, the sisters just wanted to see how much fun they could have by doing the very opposite. Getting Alexh mad became the favorite game. They even made up little songs to make her mad and sometimes they made up stories that made Alexh even madder. "But Minx, I'm trying to be responsible."

"Oh Silly Head, being responsible has everything to do with you, and nothing to do with anyone else. You're responsible for doing what's good for you. You're responsible for learning all you can to grow into the gnome you want to be. You're responsible for your feelings and for no one else's, and no one is responsible for your feelings. Even if someone tells you that you are in charge of doing something, or caring for someone, it doesn't mean that you have the right to be bossy."

Alexh thought about the struggles she had with her sisters and began to feel sad. Her nose suddenly felt itchy and Alexh sneezed. A tear rolled down her cheek and her wet skin felt a sudden cool breeze. Alexh and Minx looked up and saw a storm rolling in. "Where did that come from, and what is that terrible smell?"

The Ghillie Dhu hiding in the trees spoke to the wind, but the wind did not answer. He tried to calm the wind but it did not respond. This is no wind that I know, he thought to himself. Then the Ghillie disappeared further into the tree to hide from the strange wind that did not know him.

Minx knew where the wind came from, but decided not to tell Alexh. The breeze carried the strong odor of cooked brussel sprouts, Alexh's most unfavorite scent. "Minx, I know that smell." The wind blew hard and began to knock Alexh off her feet.

"Gnomie, follow me quickly!" as she flew as hard as she could against the breeze, ducking into a large hollow tree. Povh scurried behind her while Alexh struggled to make progress.

Alexh grabbed blades of grass and pulled herself along till she was able to get to the tree. "Minx, that storm smells like brussel sprouts! How is that possible?"

"Someone's magick I guess? It will pass. We need to keep you refocused for the whole twenty one days. So, like I was saying, no one can make you mad. I know it's hard but when you're not peptiflitter anymore it will be easy to let go of that struggle."

"Easy for you to say."

"You need to refocus to things that make you happy. Is there anything that does that?"

Alexh answered with attitude, "Yeah, things make me happy. Lots of things."

"Coolios! Lets make a list."

"Well, gliding on Povh." Alexh crinkled her nose as she thought hard to remember more. "Oh, and squishing berries between my toes!"

"Ewe!"

"It's fun. And eating acorn bread and eating blackberries, any berries really. I also like baby pooh faces and..."

"What?"

"You know, when a baby is going pooh." Alexh made a hideous face as she held her breath till her whole head became red.

Minx laughed at her and then asked in a cheeky tone, "So is there anything that you enjoy that's not disgusting?"

"I would really enjoy seeing a squirrel tied up in the vines."

"No, you can't do that."

"Oh but I can see them clearly. Just imagining them all tied up and squirming makes me laugh."
Minx scowled at Alexh and pointed her finger right at Alexh's little gnome nose and retorted, "That's not the kind of energy you want to create. If you are focused on revenge then you will just perpetuate the cycle. You have to focus on positive things. Like…"

"Like squishing berries and baby pooh faces, right?"

Minx looked exasperated. "Sure. But keep your mind open to creating fun stuff and becoming all of the cool stuff you want to see in your life. Funny at someone else's expense is just another way of perpetuating the bad stuff. The more you do this, the further you are from the reason you are here. You have a very special purpose that is in alignment with the good of all folkie everywhere."

"Really? Whoa. How do you know that?"

"Cause everyone's purpose is."

Alexh slumped back over in disappointment.

"Hey there crabby pants; that doesn't make your purpose any less special or less magickal than mine or than the most magickal beings you can imagine. You'll have more appreciation for your magick when you start to appreciate the magick in those around you."

"Oh, I do. I love your magick!"

Minx smirked at Alexh and bounced to one hip as she chirped

back again, "Not mine! You have to appreciate your sisters magick too."

Alexh rolled her eyes and purposefully yawned.

"You and your sisters should be helping each other to become more magickal."

"I don't know how. I'm not magickal like you!"

"You Silly Bean! Don't you know everyone has magick. Just because you don't know what yours is, doesn't mean it's not there. Also, no one can ever take it away from you. Even when they call you names. Only you can decide how affected you are. Once you know that, it won't matter to you anymore when people call you names or make fun of you. Would it make you mad if someone called you a purple troll?"

Alexh laughed, "Well no, I know I'm not a purple troll."

"Exactly Gnomie! You have your own magick. Don't be afraid to do crazy things to find your magick. You never know where it could be hiding. Getting creative sometimes means silly time."

"I guess so. I just don't see how being silly will help."
"Stretching your imagination is where the magick is at. You gotta trust me. I'm going to teach you how to find your magick by showing you who you really are. You should know all about the amazing things that make you so special. You become sad when you think you're not special because everything in the forest wants to know how special it is. I can tell you now that you have more amazing power than I've seen in a long time. Pixie Sneezes! The other two teams had magick too, but they let their peptiflitter control them and control the game. That's what peptiflitter does. All the magick in the forest couldn't help them if they don't have control of

30

themselves. When you can do that you don't need to control anything else. Don't let peptiflitter control your game Gnomie! Focus on what is inside of you, instead of trying to control what is outside of you."

Water began to trickle down through the hollow. It filled a large broken geode. Minx touched the water and swirled it until the image of a beautiful bird lightly shown on the surface.
"Look at the bird who has grown his beak big enough to break coconuts. All of his kind get to have the hard shell nuts that the other animals can't open. The toucan enjoys the bounty and can eat whenever he likes because there is no competition. True magick is not in competition. It is a new answer."

Loud thunder rumbled outside, holding most of Alexh's

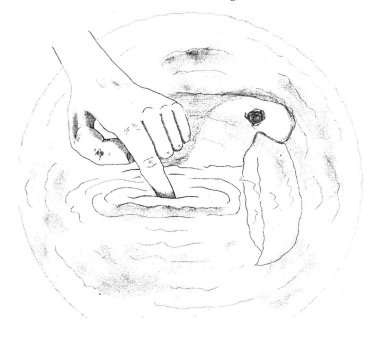

attention. She glanced at Minx and frowned.

"That's not magickal! He just has a big beak."

"What, Toucans are not magickal enough for you? You're getting spoiled. It's not going to be faerie games every day you know! It's about becoming the magick you want so much. Being different removes you from competition and places you in a position of ease. Hmf. Okay, how about the chameleon? Sparkle Magick, he's got lots of surprises!"

Minx began to move the water again until a slow moving chameleon appeared on the surface. "Of course, the chameleon began very wise. He enjoyed moving very slowly, enjoying every moment of being in the forest. He was completely in the moment. He didn't want to move fast to catch flies, and he didn't want to run from owls and other large birds. Being a wise master and being in the moment, he turned within. His strong desire was to become hidden and to see everything going on around him, without having to even move his head.

He first taught his body to change its chemistry so that he produced more of a hormone[2] that binds with the skin. That hormone makes his skin change all different pretty colors! Then he taught his skin to have different types of receivers that change the colors in his skin depending on the mood he is in. He chooses his mood. Then he slowly stretched out the muscles around his eyes so that he can see all the way around his head. His funny looking eyes easily move independently of each other. He was also able to teach his brain to understand what he see's through the two independent eyes. Now all chameleons are born knowing how to produce these hormones and control their skin color. Do you see how important it is to know how to control yourself and your chemistry?"

"I guess. Can I learn to change my skin Minx?

"You could, but then I'd get to call you a funny purple troll!" Minx said tickling Alexh. "Aren't you happy being a gnome?"

"I want to be a pixie so that I can fly all by myself."

"Oh like the gliders. They just wanted to fly too." Minx churned the water again to reveal funny little animals with markings similar to Povh, but without the great folds of extra skin on their sides. "They were cute fury animals who wanted to become something else, just like you. They had great little hands and enjoyed running around in the dark and sometimes the light. They often watched the birds glide gracefully through the air and longed to be able to glide through the trees. They would often pretend to have great wings, and would practice jumping to branches that were further and further apart. The forest honors such a deep desire and gave these little guys the opportunity to change. They would stretch with all their might in order to leap just a little further. They

---

2   Hormones are magickal things running through a body all the time. See Glossary.

trusted that they would land safely, and had no fear of these great leaps. Over time the skin on their sides, called patagium began to stretch, allowing them to glide further and further. Now gliders like your friend Povh are born with this extra skin on their sides." she says as she tugs and plays with the folds of Povh's furry body. "Of course they glide further with young gnomes like you riding."

"But I don't ride very well. I wish I had real magick, so that I could wake up with great big wings, like you and the butterfly."

"You should try being grateful for the ability to ride as well as you do, the ability to see so well at night and day, the great family you have and the fact that you have the ability to be a great animal healer someday. Being a gnome has fantastic magickal possibilities if that is the magick you choose. No one else but gnomes have this great combination of gifts. You're also more magickal than you think. You create stuff all the time. It's just because you've been so mad, you create bad stuff. You managed to totally destroy your birthday cake every year for three years! That's pretty powerful."

"Really? I'm powerful?"

"Absolutely! Every time you create a coincident or when you hear from someone just after thinking of them, or even when something bad happens to you over and over. It's all your magickal ability to create. You create what's inside of you. So when your insides are full of friction; you create friction. Now do you see what a powerful being you are?"

"No. You're telling me that the thing I'm trying to get rid of is my magick?"

"No Silly Bean! You are working at getting rid of your peptiflitter. Your brain gets used to releasing certain types of chemicals called pepti's[3]. There's about a bagillion different combinations you could be making in your brain right now. If you are in control of yourself, and learning to stay in your happy magickal place, then you create amazing things. Its great surprises every day for you, Gnomie! If you put all of your magickal energy into being mad, then you produce pepti's [3]that are released, bond to your cells, and make you a magnet for things you don't like and they can make you get sick or just feel really sad."

Alexh just stared blankly at Minx with deep confusion. "I don't know if I can learn all of this. Why did you decide to help me anyway? Did you just feel sad for me?"

"Absolutely not! I think beings like you are really amazing and total sparkle magick. Of course, it's really entertaining to see what crazy thing you're going to make happen next. But I'm honored to teach you. Sometimes a really powerful being is born to help everyone else to see. They purposely forget how amazing they really are, so that they can be negative and allow the strangest things to happen to them. They make a great sacrifice to live all tied up in peptiflitter. Other's see the strange stuff that happens, and begin to expect to see the bad things happen to the unlucky one all the time. They finally begin to realize that through their feelings and actions, it is possible to effect everything around them. There are also beings who are always very lucky. But you, Alexh, are the very brave one."

Alexh's jaw dropped, and tears came to her eyes. "No one has ever called me brave before. I think it's the first time you've called me Alexh too." She smiled and gave Minx a very big warm gnome hug.

"Does this mean you're going to stop calling me weird

---

3 More wonky magickal stuff that runs around in your body. See Glossary Hormones.

 Majick

names?"

"No chance Snot Head. That's just the way I roll."

The loud thundering and harsh winds were replaced by the welcoming sounds of birds chirping. "Wow, that blew over quickly." Alexh stepped out of the tree hollow and took a deep cleansing breath. "It doesn't smell like brussel sprouts anymore either. That's good, because I really don't like the smell of brussel sprouts at all."

Minx giggled, but chose not to discuss the weird smell. "There are a lot of things we need to discuss. Before we can change your chemistry I need you to understand your connection to the forest. You also need to know that positive focus is way stronger than negative focus. It's stronger and more creative every time. The positive focus of any folkie is like the veins that the forest runs through."

"Okay. I believe you, but why?

"Because the forest is the source of all creativity and its connection to your heart strengthens the magick that you are. Although you are a powerful force all on your own, that combination triggers an energy that creates changes you couldn't imagine."

"Do you mean that when bad stuff happens, it's all my fault?"

"No Gnomie. Don't start worrying about where to place the blame."

"But that's what you're saying, it's all my fault!"
"No that's not it! Now Listen."

Alexh's eyes began to well up because she was feeling the blame for all of the bad things that happened.

"No Gnomie." Minx caressed Alexh's long beautiful hair. "The forest is a current of possibilities. Even if you had some terrible wish or intent it is not in alignment with what the forest has in mind for you. The forest will mold and change your negative focus into a lesson for you. It holds you in a place of positive possibilities even when you have not learned to do this yet. Nothing is your fault."

"But if I'm always creating, and it's all bad luck, didn't I create bad things?"

"Very few gnomes have learned to control the energies. The energies are teachers, who sometimes bring harsh lessons to show you what you are doing to yourself on the inside. The harm you do on the inside is way more harmful than stuff on the outside."

"But I've also heard about really horrible things that happened to other gnomes, like a fire or death."

"Alexh, you are a very old and very wise being who chose to forget all of your wisdom while completing certain promises with yourself and others. When a gnome is born they choose to explore places they have never been, to do things they have never done and to understand things they felt a strong need to understand. When something really terrible happens, it has something to do with this promise. Perhaps it is to push them to a place where they could understand a situation better, to become more compassionate or to teach others around them. Powerful beings often choose the path less followed because they understand the importance of all lessons. I know that sounds harsh. The reasons for such things to happen are endless and only that one single gnome knows why, and they may not know the answer until their spirit is done being in this world."

"I don't understand. That's a really complicated answer and it

still hurts to know that terrible things happen."

"It's a really complicated question that has no simple answers. All I can tell you is that some day you will know why you chose to forget how powerful you are, and someday those other gnomes will also know why they made such a sacrifice. You must just know that you and those others are great powerful beings on the other side. They did what was best for all concerned. For now, it is important that you explore this opportunity to be you and know that you are no less loved by the forest than the lucky gnomes, or the gnomes with straight teeth or the gnomes who glide better."

Alexh didn't look any happier. She wanted to fix everything she knew about the forest, but somehow she knew that it was not her right to fix things. "Minx, it's not fair. I still wish I could fix it all. Sometimes I think that if I didn't have to deal with certain other gnomes that I would be a better creator."

"You are always doing your part to create change when you act from the heart. Someday all the faerie folk will be in harmony with each other again, because of the role you play in the forest. Every time you act in generosity and sincerity for others you gain knowledge and you create more balance."

"Okay, say I finally have unlimited magick. How do I know when it's okay to help and when it's not okay?"

"The forest will be in alignment for you to help. It will be easy. All that you need will only be there when the timing is right and you understand your role. You are the magick in your life and so are others around you. The lessons will always come from the strangest places. It is important that you understand that you are as magickal as the acorn or the breeze or the tiniest ant. The more you learn about yourself and others, the easier it will be to know what to do. Does that make sense?"

"If I say that it does, will you teach me how to be more magickal already?"

"Oh Gnomie, you're more magick than I can deal with some days!"

As the storm began to fade Alexh noticed a tuft of grey and purple poking out from under the brush just outside of the hollow. She reached out to touch it but then the large bird-like creature bounced out at her. It ran about her until the momentum of being startled wore off. Then it began to make strange little chirps. They were the funniest sounds she had ever heard. Alexh enjoyed the sounds until the creature got closer and began to jump up and down repeating sharper tones. "Weird bird." She said as she tossed a sweet blackberry into her mouth.

Minx giggled at Alexh, "That's a booghopper. I think you should give him a treat for all the nice chirping he did for you."

"Why? He can get to the berries himself." Alexh said as she tossed another berry into her mouth."

"Okay then." Minx giggled as she watched the booghopper get increasing louder until he finally nipped Alexh's knee.

"Ouch!" she yelled as she turned to run away. But the moment she was faced the other way, the booghopper nipped her hinie. "Ouch!", Alexh continued as she threw the berries at him.

The booghopper then made cheerful chirps again, disappearing into the forest, leaving Alexh curled up in a tree with her brow furrowed. "Why did he do that? Stupid bird thing."

"That's how he gets what he needs. Everything in the forest

gets what it needs in its own way. This creature counts on the kindness of folkies."

Alexh's pouting soon turned to embarrassment as she didn't realize she was supposed to be kind. She turned to Povh and began to roll around and play with him. This is what Povh most enjoys with Alexh.

The three spent the day dashing from one tree to the next. They played tag and hide and seek, snacked on sweet fruit and enjoyed watching other animals. Minx told Alexh about sea otters who can remain pregnant from four to nine months by delaying implantation so that the baby is born during months of warmer weather. She also told her about certain frogs that are able to change their gender from female to male if needed. They discussed animals who put their bodies to sleep for the winter and cuttlefish who change their color for protection.

Alexh noticed a strange spider spinning a web. She thought that the web spinning was a beautiful craft and wondered how it worked. "Minx, how does the spider walk around on the web without getting stuck?"

"That's a fantastical question! The spider can control its chemistry too. They first produce a nonsticky silk for their design. Once that part is all finished they change the recipe by changing their chemistry. Then they can lay sticky silk in

a spiral. The spider knows which is which, but no one else does."

Alexh rolled her eyes, because she had heard enough about animals who had better control over their chemistry than she did. She really wanted to become a different gnome. "Come on Povh, let's see how high we can go!" He bounced from branch to branch high in a beautiful pine tree. When he leaped Alexh felt her stomach contract and get a little queasy. Then wind blew them out of control and Alexh became terrified. Neither Alexh nor Povh could see where they were headed. When Alexh opened her eyes they were caught by more tangled vines. She never thought she'd be grateful for big tangled up vines. However her relief quickly turned to aggravation as the vines began to tighten around them as they struggled to get loose.

The Ghillie Dhu was watching them struggle and sent a message on the wind to the vines. He told them to untangle around the little gnome and gently let her drop to another branch. Then he blew a spell upon the wind to carry her and Povh safely and swiftly through the trees. Alexh began to gain confidence in her riding and finally started to feel connected with her glider.

They landed in a clump of tree flowers so that she could properly snuggle with him. "Wow Povh, you're awesome!"

Minx joined them. "Yeppers, all ya gotta do is stretch your limits. You can't let a day go by that your not doing this, cause you never know when your magick's gonna kick in."

As the skies darkened, Minx began to teach Alexh all about how her little body worked and why she feels so emotional. Alexh talked about the weird bad luck she's had and about what she was thinking and doing at the time the bad luck struck. This is a good exercise for any peptiflitter gnome and although Minx doesn't always do what's right, this is a good

thing for Alexh right now.

"I want to keep working on this all night!" Alexh jumped up as if she just got her second wind. But Minx sat her back down into the nest of petals and soft green leaves.

"You have another big day ahead of you tomorrow, so you could start now by just dreaming yourself into your magick. Sweet dreams Silly Bean."

CHAPTER 4

Dont let the ogres steal your teachers

Alexh began to dream of being home with her sisters. She was racing to a river and plunged first into the water. It felt so rewarding to be first. But Alexh's pleasure suddenly turned to struggle as she found herself unable to stay afloat. This had never happened before. Swimming generally came naturally to Alexh. So why was it so difficult to stay afloat? Alexh began to grab sticks floating by, but they could not support her weight.

Sam and Megan saw Alexh struggling and reached out to her from an overhanging branch.

Alexh pulled away. "I can do it!" She didn't want her sisters to think that they could do anything better than her. It had been a constant struggle for Alexh to make sure that she's the best at everything. In fact she worried about not being the best at swimming, gliding, gathering, hiding, playing

and everything else. Why was it so important? Sam yelled,
"Lean back and spread your arms across the water, you'll float
better!" Alexh yelled, "I know what I'm doing!" Now she
had to figure out how to float without spreading her arms and
depending on them. It would feel tragic to take the advice of
her sister. What would that lead to? Then Sam might start
giving advice all the time. Since Alexh liked to give all of the
advice, it would be miserable receiving advice from her two
sisters who were supposed to be the followers. Alexh felt like
a leader, and just couldn't stand to take direction at all.

As she continued to struggle a larger branch floated just
within her grasp, which carried Alexh far down the river. She
watched Sam and Meagan appear smaller and smaller until
she could no longer see them.
By the time Alexh could finally reach the shore she was in
another part of the forest. It was very unfamiliar. As she
began to wander back up the river she came across three ogres.
The largest of the three was very angry. Seeing this immense
creature so hot tempered was a very scary thing for a tiny
gnome. Alexh hurried into a bush, where she could watch
safely.

The biggest ogre was yelling about the broken wheel on a cart
they were sharing. He had to unload all of their treasures and
struggle with trying to repair the cart. He began yelling at
the two smaller ogres, "If you wouldn't have hit that rock we
wouldn't be here trying to fix this cart! Move out of my way!
Why do I have to do everything myself?!"

One of the smaller ogres said, "I have an idea. If we just…"

But the biggest ogre yelled in his face, "Do you think you
know better than me? I am older than you, and I've done
more than you and I've seen more than you! Are you trying to
show me up?"

The two smaller ogres shook their heads no.

Some time had passed and the angry ogre gave up on fixing the wheel. He threw his things into a blanket and flung the wad of treasures over his back. "I'm sick of that stupid cart. It breaks down all the time and it's useless!"

The two smaller ogres waited till he was completely out of sight. Then they worked quickly to fix the wheel and hurried down another trail with the cart all to themselves.

Alexh woke up staring up into the thick foliage above.

"What's got your wheels turning freckle face?" Minx asked as she brushed Alexh's hair with her fingers.
"I had a weird dream." And Alexh told her the whole dream.

"Yeppers, dreams are great teachers. You draw the appropriate lessons, right on time. No different than the appropriate teachers when you're awake."

"How's that?

"Think about how your sisters were trying to teach you to swim. You should always let others help you."

"But I already know how to swim. I don't know why I couldn't swim while I was dreaming. I just know that I didn't need their help." Alexh rolled her eyes and crossed her arms.

"But you seem to think that they can never teach you anything. Isn't it a lot of pressure trying to do everything better? Why do you have to? I thought you already learned that everyone has their own magick."

"Yeah, but this is just every day stuff. I don't want them to think they're better than me."

Minx put her hands on both sides of Alexh's face. "You need to learn that teachers come to you in all shapes, sizes and forms. Never ever let the ogre cheat you out of a lesson.

Dreams are great teachers, just like the dream about your sisters. You dreamed about ogres fighting over a cart, and also the ogre that is inside of you.

The ogre is a part of you that can steal your lessons from you. It makes you forget to be the student and the teacher at all times. You should never let the ogre become more powerful than you. It is a kind of fear of not being good enough, that causes you to act like you are better than others around you. Every time a teacher approaches you, ogre puffs itself up and hides the lesson from you. It can be a very nasty aspect. In your dream, the largest ogre didn't believe that a younger ogre could teach him anything. He was also not willing to sacrifice his inner ogre in order to let the two younger ones contribute to the answer. Sometimes it takes a fresh perspective to see the answer. Sometimes it takes many perspectives, from many unexpected places before the best solution can be created."

"Minx, you don't understand. If I let one of my sisters help me, they will make fun of me. They will think its okay to tell me what to do all the time."

"They probably don't like it anymore than you do. Try to realize that it doesn't matter what they think. The only thing that really matters is how much knowledge you are able to gain. Never think that there is a being that has nothing to teach you. The wisest beings know that a mind that is ready to learn will attract more lessons. You should cherish every opportunity no matter where it comes from."

"But I think I'd rather drown than let my sister's call me stupid."

45

"You absolutely have to let go of worrying about what anyone else thinks. If you don't, that ogre will eat away at you forever. You don't understand how big and unpredictable the ogre can be. Ogres can be terribly sneaky and they rob you of everything. They are bigger than trolls and nastier than trows and they come from something even nastier, FEAR! Sometimes the best way to overcome a fear is to think of the worst possible thing that could happen, and then realize that even that isn't so bad."

Alexh exclaims, "What? Are you crazy? You don't understand at all!"

"What's the worst possible thing that could happen?"
"They could torture me with name calling and they could think that they're better than me. They could treat me like a baby!"

"So, what else?"

"That would be awful! I would be so mad. I couldn't stand it."

"But what someone else thinks, doesn't change you. You need to have control over what is inside of you. Sometimes growing stronger and wiser can hurt. Sacrificing your ogre is probably the most painful lesson you'll ever have. It's also the most important and empowering lesson. If you don't sacrifice it, it will rule over you, control you, and keep you from becoming the magickal gnomie we are working so hard for you to become. You simply have to do it. You have no problem learning from me. Why is that?"

Alexh had been rolling her eyes and watching the birds above her. She only turned her head briefly to respond, "Because you're smart and I trust you."

"Coolios! Understand you just need to know that you're smart too. You have to trust that you are full of magick waiting to be discovered."

Alexh closed her eyes and groaned.

"You said that you trust me. I know I'm right about you. If I cannot teach you how to overcome the ogre, then it will continue to come after you for your whole life. You can never escape a lesson and you will not be able to overcome your peptiflitter. Haven't you ever met a being that can't understand why the same things continues happening to them?"

"Yeah, that would be me."

Minx grabbed Alexh's face with a dramatic sense of urgency. "Overcoming the ogre is your only hope."

"Okay, I trust you, geez. How do I start to overcome my ogre?"

"Coolios! I'm so glad you're willing to do this, because I need a day off."

"A day off? What do you mean a day off?"

"I'm saying that you need a different teacher today."

"But Minx!"

"Oh, don't worry about a thing. I plan to leave you in capable hands." Minx faded away and then appeared again just behind Alexh. "Ta Da!" As she points to the baby platypus. "Yeppers, I brought him here from far away. His mom's not feeling well today, so you're the babysitter. Learn all you can! And don't forget to tame the nasty ogre."

Alexh yelled, "What! No!" but it was too late. Minx had disappeared

CHAPTER 5

Unexpected Teachers

Minx had left Alexh stuck babysitting. The little gnome looked at the strange creature she abruptly became responsible for. She had no idea where to begin. She had never seen a platypus before, and didn't know what it was.

The Ghillie Dhu had still been watching. He was really sad to see Minx disappear. He knew the only way to see her again was to continue to tail Alexh. He also began to like Alexh and wanted to see her successful at overcoming her peptiflitter. Alexh still had not learned to listen to the animals. This could make taking care of this large weird animal really difficult. She also had not been able to learn from Povh, who could probably teach her a lot.

The Ghillie Dhu decided to cast another spell for Alexh. He tainted some berries right next to her with a tonic that would allow her to hear the animals for a day. Alexh noticed the berries and ate a few and threw the rest into Povh's mouth. These berries would allow clear communication between her and the animals she needed to understand. They would provide mental translation of whatever the animal was trying to communicate; though she would still need to comprehend more than the words that are conveyed through this tonic.

Once the tonic had run through her system, Alexh began to look at her situation. She said to herself out loud, "What kind of animal is this?"

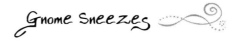

"My mom calls me Ned."

Alexh yelled, "Eek!" And fell back into a bush.
"How did you do that? Why can I hear you?"

Ned began to cry, as young animals do.
Alexh felt sad for him and tried to comfort the baby animal,
which was much bigger than her. She carefully patted him on
the bill and smiled at him. He soon noticed her trying to help.

"Well Ned, what am I supposed to do with you?"

"I'm hungry now, so feed me." He said in a cheerful tone.

Povh rushed in and said, "Feed me too. If it's feeding time,
feed me too!"

Alexh fell over again. "This must be some magick that Minx
has done. Hold on Povh, you just had berries. Go chase some
grasshoppers, or something"

Povh reluctantly backed away and began to hunt for
grasshoppers in the tall green grass.

Alexh noticed he looked a bit put out, but she felt like taking
care of one thing at a time. This large baby animal appeared
to be a bit more than what she could handle. She gradually
moved closer and asked, "What do Ned's eat?"

"My mom fed me milk."

"Eek! Nope I don't have any of that for you." Alexh jumped
back and approached again from the side. Povh decided to
help out with the big weird animal. He watched how Alexh
tugged and poked and examined every inch of Ned. Povh
began to mimic Alexh by sniffing around and poking all over
the baby animal too.

"Certainly there is some clue about what to feed a Ned." Alexh nodded with certainty at Povh.

Povh tugged on Ned's side to see if the skin could stretch. He wasn't sure how friendly the new animal might be, so he barked a bit whenever Ned looked back at him. He wanted Ned to know who's boss, in case there was any question.

Alexh started worrying about getting eaten if she didn't find food right away. She was very careful to stay away from Ned's large beak.

Povh began pulling on the animals' beak, "What a weird beak! It's all bendy. I don't think you can crunch up nuts or seeds or anything. Guess you'll have to eat worms!"

Alexh thought that was really funny, because even Povh won't eat worms unless all the fruit is gone. He's supposed to like

50

worms, but he's a bit spoiled.

Alexh scooped up a worm from the soft wet dirt. "Open your mouth and I'll put it in."

Ned muffled, "No! It looks yucky. I don't want it."

"Well, you have duck feet. I could push you into the water and we can see if you can swim out and catch fish." Alexh looked very excited about that idea. She was starting to enjoy being in control again; probably a little too much.

"No, I'm afraid of the water. What if I don't know how to swim?"

"Then worms it is!" Alexh began shoving the big squishy worm into Ned's mouth. It twisted and wrestled with her a bit, but she was determined to get the weird creature fed. "How's the worm?"

"Slirp…hmmpf. Not as good as milk, but I could get used to them."

"Yay!" Alexh continued pushing worms into Ned's mouth until he couldn't eat anymore.

"Hey Ned, let's go on an adventure! Povh and I are great adventurers and we're inviting you along."

"To where?"

"I don't know, maybe to the other side of the lake. I bet there's a lot of neat stuff over there."

"No way. I have short stubby legs and tender feet."

Povh raced up panting, "I bet there are a lot of really cool things to eat over there."

Ned cocked his head to one side. "Ok."

Alexh, Povh and Ned began their journey around the lake. Alexh had ordered Povh to be lookout for any trouble ahead. He would often stop to scurry up a tree and play lookout. He climbed to the highest branches to see as far as he could, although he was really hoping to see Minx. Ned didn't mind stopping at all. He needed the rest and enjoyed talking to the plants and trees. Alexh thought he was just silly. She listened really hard but never heard the trees answer.

Ned laid his head against a smooth tree root. "Yep tree, these are my new friends Alexh and Povh. Alexh is really bossy, but she feeds me nice fat worms. Oh yes you're right, she's really smart like that."

Alexh blushed. She didn't believe that Ned was hearing anything other than his imagination, but she did appreciate being complimented, even if only by the imagination of this silly creature.

Povh continued to scurry around in the tree, pretending to do important things. He climbed to a very high spot in a tree that gave him just the right angle to see lots of different berry bushes way on the other side of the lake. This was a very big lake. "Wow! Now that's the spot we need to get to." He looked down at Ned still resting his head on the tree root. "At the pace Ned walks it will take a very long time to get there, but still well worth the trip. I hope Minx gets back soon." Povh glided back down from the tree. "Alexh, Ned! There are tons of sweet berries on the other side of the lake. All different kinds!"

"Yay!" Alexh jumped up and down.
"Yay. What are berries?" asked Ned.

Alexh wrapped her arms around Ned's big head, "They are just the sweetest yummiest things ever. And that's a real good thing Ned. Maybe that's something you can eat."
Povh climbed onto Ned's back. "You're gonna like berries."

"Okay, but I'm hungry now."

Alexh did her best to find a few fat worms in the mud next the water. Povh found a few stray seeds to share. It's a good thing that gliders are such great gatherers.

Ned continued to walk at his slow pace, with his head swinging back and forth. Alexh and Povh played in the trees and would glide just ahead to wait for Ned to catch up. Ned watched the way Alexh and Povh glided around in the trees. He thought to himself, "They are so brave to look out for me."

Alexh wondered why Ned swung his head back and forth like that. It's very peculiar to watch. She didn't know that this was his special way of communicating with all of the forest. He can pick up waves of movement and even the conversations between the trees. He could feel where Alexh and Povh where in the trees above him. He could hear the secrets being told among the smallest elementals and the gossip among the birds. As Ned worked his way through his adventure the fears he had slipped away as they were replaced with the peace he felt in every living thing.

"No tree, Alexh never talks to trees or plants. I think she doesn't hear you. Awe, well thank you. I think you're really handsome too....."

Alexh stopped paying attention to Ned. She was beginning to worry about being without Minx. She nervously glanced in all directions as she rode Povh up the side of a large old oak. Terrible thoughts began to cloud her mind.

There is no way to get him up a tree and the idea of sleeping on the ground with all of the scary things that run around at night was not at all appealing to Alexh. She unmounted Povh and let him run up a branch going in another direction. Then she curled up into a tiny hollow, hoping that no one could hear or see her.

Alexh quietly spoke aloud to herself, "What am I going to do with him? He's got yam legs and stupid feet. He can't fly and he's scared of the water. He's the weirdest looking thing I've ever seen. He's so big I can't figure out how I'm supposed to be responsible for him. I can't even believe that big thing is a baby." She was allowing her perspective to be tainted by her impatience. "Ishu!" Alexh wiped her nose and leaned back to relax against the tree. Tiny ants started to get into her clothing. All at once, they began to bite. Alexh screamed, then sneezed again, ishu! Povh came swooping down to her and carried her to the lake, where he quickly dropped her.

The biting was over, but now she was wet and worried that she may not completely dry before nightfall. Now she had the chore of wringing out all of her cloths as Ned continued to rest his head against the trunk of a large tree.

Ned had been communicating with his friends, the trees when Alexh was complaining about him. Although Alexh was talking very quietly to herself, Ned heard everything. He felt really sad and useless... and hungry again. "Tree, why did she say those mean things? I wish I was a tiny nimble animal like Povh but I'm just not. I'm so sad." The tree whispered to Ned that he is very different from all of the other creatures in the forest because he has very different kinds of magick. Trees sometimes know the future because they are very old and the best listeners in the whole forest. Ned continued to listen to the trees. They told him that it is important for Alexh to understand what happiness is. "Happiness can not be found, because it is not a thing. You do not need to look for

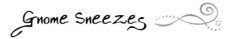

it. Happiness is a part of you that requires nourishment. The trees continued to teach Ned about happiness and encouraged him to relay the message when he felt it was appropriate. They also told him to not worry about what Alexh has said out of her fears and worry. They explained to Ned that he had his own magick that it would soon be discovered. They did not want to ruin the surprise. Ned had come to trust the advice of the trees, so he felt comfort in all of the things that were told to him.

Alexh noticed that it was beginning to get dark and they still hadn't figured out what to do with Ned. She and Povh glided down to talk to him. "Ned, I can't get you up the tree and it's getting late. I'm wondering how much longer it will be before Minx gets here."

"Oh don't worry, she'll be here in a few days."

"What! Did she tell you that?"

"No I heard it from the trees."

Alexh laughed, because she thought Ned was just silly.

"I heard she got side tracked and can't make it. But one tree said that we will learn a lot, and it will be okay."

Alexh was still laughing. "Well okay Ned, but we need to find a place for you to sleep."

"I used to sleep in a hole with my mom. I miss her"

Alexh hugged him and thought about her family. "Well I miss my mom too. We lived under a tree."

Povh suddenly pounced on the two of them. "That's what we need! A tree with a hole big enough to get you into." Povh

scurried back up the tree and scouted out the area until he found just the right tree. He told Ned and Alexh where to start walking and glided ahead to check it out. He also found lots of fresh soft leaves to put in the bottom for everyone to sleep on.

By the time Ned and Alexh made it to the tree they were very, very tired. Alexh pushed a few more worms into Ned's mouth and watched him fall asleep.

Povh was still wide awake as gliders can be at night. He jumped around in the trees until he saw a strange little animal enter their tree! Povh raced down and saw the creature running back out screaming, "No, no, no! Won't do, won't do! Don 't like it, don't like it!"

Alexh came running out of the tree. "Shhhhhhh! He's sleeping." Alexh whispered loudly to the creature."

"Sleeping! Sleeping you say?! This is my house, mine! Get him out, out now!" the fast talking little creature piped in high pitch chatter.

Alexh thought about her predicament. "Well, I don't like to wake him because he's always hungry. He eats little animals you know. What kind of little animal are you?"

"Ack! No way, no way! Make it go away!" the creature screeched in a very fast voice.

"Well he likes me. I'm sure that it will be okay if we share the tree for the night. Especially if maybe you have some nice berries?"

"No berries, no berries at all."

"Troll Snot." Mumbled Alexh.

"What was that?" asked the strange creature.

"Oh just an expression I picked up from my friend Minx."

"Minx! Why didn't you say so? A friend of Minx is a friend of Tikidu. That's me, Tikidu. Brought me here from the other world she did. I'm a senewmoni. The only one in this world, I am. Only me. and yes, that's right one night and one night only. Then you and your hungry friend can find another tree!"

"It's a deal! Thanks for the help. We've been waiting for Minx…"

"Oh yes, trixie little Minx. Got herself into trouble with the Ghille Dhu, she did. That's what I heard."

"Oh my!"

"Oh, no need to worry. Just a little faerie feuding. She'll be back in a few days. I'm sure of it. Now get some sleep. I'll not be tolerating you and your furry friend scampering about my tree all night."

The odd little Tikidu carefully squeezed past Ned and went to sleep high up in the hollow. Alexh snuggled up next to Ned and Povh on the floor of the hollow. Eventually Alexh fell into a deep sleep.

The night's peaceful sounds suddenly became silent. A strange sound began to grow closer. Thud, crash, thud crash, thud crash! As the sound became continuously louder there was growling and a horrifying cackling. Alexh and Tikidu were awakened by the racket and the terrible odor that seemed to be getting worse. "What is that?" Alexh asked Tikidu.

Tikidu began to nervously run circles around the inner tree. "Only one mean, mean creature in the forest with that smell.

Unexpected Teachers

It's a Fachan, for sure."

Alexh remembered the ugly creature from the faerie games. Suddenly they didn't seem so funny. "Oh no! What will he do?"

Tikidu exclaimed, "They are known to be terribly frightful. So frightful! Scaring some to death, they do!"

Alexh wondered how that was possible, but she remembered how strong and mean she saw the Fachan get during the game. She did not want to face this creature.

Other small animals ran into the tree and scurried up to safety. Povh had scurried up to be with all of the other animals. All but Ned, who was still sleeping on the ground.

Thud crash, thud crash! Then the Fachan flung back his mace and hit the tree with it. The tiny animals inside became anxious. They wanted to run out of the top of the tree.

Tikidu held them all back, "Stay calm, stay calm! You'll be making his day you will. No running out into his view!

The tiny birds and animals grew restless. The loud banging was making everyone crazy.

With all of the noise, Ned was beginning to wake up. He was very scared because he didn't know what the commotion was all about. He began to growl aloud clicking growl and then shook his head back and forth.

The loud sounds from the outside became still. Ned kept shaking his head and growling. He could hear the tree telling him to be brave. Still partly asleep, he growled louder and louder.

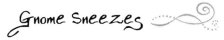

A dark hairy hand lunged through the opening. Ned was faced the other way and never saw it enter. He only felt the firm grip around his hind leg. Then a loud horrible frightening scream came from the Fachan as he jerked his arm back and suddenly disappeared.

Ned collapsed in exhaustion. Tikidu dropped to the floor level and began to examine the tiny barb on Ned's hind leg. "Ah, venom, it is! Your friend has many secrets I see."

Alexh dropped down to Ned and looked at the tiny barb as well. "What do you mean venom? Like a snake?"

"Oh yes, like a snake he is. Shoots venom into his predator. Lucky to have him here tonight, we are. Hahaha! Old nasty face must be hot about this! Hahaha! You'll be staying here with Tikidu anytime you'd like Ned. Forever welcome! Won't be sticken that arm in this tree ever again, old nasty face!" Tikidu laughed and made his way back up into his sleeping nook.

Alexh and Povh praised Ned and stroked his sheen fur until he fell back to sleep. The clicking snore he made then lulled everyone else back to sleep as the forest gradually brought back the peaceful sounds of the night.

The next morning many of the other animals that lived in that part of the forest came to thank Ned for his special magick that frightened the Fachan away. It was about time that something scared him away for a change and it was in the forests own timing that it happen that night.

Ned enjoyed all of the attention he was getting. The birds chirped for him and the small animals danced in the trees in gratitude for the great thing that he did.

Alexh was beginning to feel a bit in Ned's shadow. "Come on

Ned, we still have our adventure ahead."

"On an adventure you are?" Tikidu asked.

"Oh yes, it's our secret adventure. "Alexh added, not wishing to give away their big secret.

An older bird cooed, "Don't go too far around this lake. There is certain danger on the other side of this lake. I have felt it flying over and there is no sound of the forest there."

Ned looked very worried, "Wha…"

But Alexh grabbed his rubbery beak, "Oh no, not going that far. It's just our little secret adventure."

Tikidu had been racing back and forth across the branches of the tree. His nervous behavior reminded Alexh of a squirrel, though he looked nothing like one. "Now don't you be forgettin where you found me. I'll be here. Here when you pass this way again."

"Will do Tikidu. We're off!" Alexh lead the way as she turned down the path.

Povh pounced around in the trees above and Alexh walked with Ned. They continued their journey as all of the little animals waved goodbye in their own special ways. It seemed no sooner than they were out of sight, Ned reminded Alexh to feed him. They walked into the muddy area next to the water.

"Look Ned, I don't mind feeding you but look at my little hands. They were not made for digging."

Ned looked at his hands and wondered what they were made for. This made him really sad. Then he covered his eyes with his hands and buried his nose into the mud and cried. Alexh

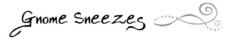

stroked his back. "I'm sorry. We'll figure out what your hands do and everything else."

Ned spoke in a muffled tone because his snout was in the mud, "You promise?"

"Yes. I know we can figure this out somehow."

"Yay!" Ned pulled his nose up from the mud and the mud flew up into the air and landed way behind him.

Alexh was astonished. "How did you do that?"

"I don't know."

"Do it again."

Ned pushed his beak into the mud and pulled up another big blob of mud, which this time landed on Alexh.
"Augh!" she yelped.

"Sorry."

"That's okay. Just keep doing it until you find your own worms."

Alexh waded in the water to rinse the mud away. She was a bit miffed about having to be cold and wet this time of the morning. "You know it's really hard to be in a good mood when everything happens to me." She grumped and groaned. Povh ignored her crabbing while he chased and feasted on grasshoppers.

Ned was beginning to feel full and ignored as Povh stole one of his worms. Ned didn't mind at all. "There's plenty of food here. Do you want some Alexh?" as he held out a really wiggly one at the end of his beak.

Alexh snapped, "No, I don't eat worms. I'm not going to be happy until we get to those berries."

Ned remembered the conversation he had with the trees about happiness. "Alexh, why is it so important to get to the berries over there? If we look around in the forest over here we can probably find really good stuff for you to eat."

With that, Povh began scouting for food, though he's not a very good judge of gnome food.

Ned rolled over onto one side, completely satisfied. Then he touted something strange. "You can find the berries but you cannot find happiness."

Alexh looked at him dumbfounded. "What does that mean? I'm working hard at this. How could you say that Ned?"

Ned said proudly, "I heard it from the trees. They said that there are messages that I need to relay to you."

Alexh still felt that his ability to hear trees was nonsense. "Well, your tree friends are all wrong. I will certainly find happiness."

Ned calmly began to relay the message, "Happiness is not something you can find, because it is not a thing. It is not separate from you. No matter how hard you look for it, you will not find it. It is a part of you that needs to be nourished. "

Alexh laughed, "Haha, that's what the berries are for silly-head."

"It needs to be nourished with appreciation for all that is in the now. Appreciation for others and for the goodness that flows to you."

Alexh nodded her head back and forth and mimicked Ned as she rolled her eyes. She didn't like being handed wisdom from the one she was babysitting.

"Then you experience the love you feel when you are sharing with others"

"I'm not eating your worms."

"You also feed it wisdom through listening. It's very important to pay attention to the lessons that flow to you. You should also appreciate them. Even if they sometimes hurt a little." His voice trailed off.

"Ned, I know you mean well, but I'm cold, wet and hungry. I just want to get there now!"

Povh jumped onto Ned. "Maybe you can find us berries? Please ask your tree friends."

"I heard the whispering of a berry bush around the willow that still has some berries right now."

Alexh giggled, "You silly Ned. Trees and bushes can't talk. I've been listening and they never answer you."

"I feel them talking. When I wave my head back and forth, I can feel the trees talking, I can feel Povh jumping around in the trees and I can feel everything communicating."

Alexh sat very still and couldn't feel anything.

"Just go around the willow and you'll see a bush with berries."

Alexh walked around the willow and saw a nice big bush with tiny black yummy berries. She couldn't believe her eyes. She and Povh ate them quickly. They giggled and got all blackberry messy; though neither could get much dirtier

than they already had gotten from the journey so far. Alexh looked at her soiled cloths and decided that she had more dry area than wet area and it will dry as they walk in the sun. The urgency to get to food had dropped away and then the other side of the lake did not appear to be as far away as it did previously.

Alexh licked her hands clean and thought more about Ned's magickal ability to hear the trees. "How the heck did you learn to do that thing with the trees?"

"I told you. I just feel everything communicate and move."

"Maybe that's what I'm supposed to learn from you. Minx said to keep an eye out for my teachers, but I was ignoring your magick."

"That's my magick?"

"Yep, everyone has magick."

"The trees told me that we're going to find out all about our own magick."

Ned tried to snuggle up to Povh, nearly squishing him. "I think you're very brave all the time. You are also beautiful when you glide. I can feel you gliding above me and the trees think you're beautiful too."

Alexh felt left out, so she climbed onto the two. "Maybe I can teach you something Ned. You really do have funny duck feet. I think they are made for water. Why don't you let me teach you how to swim?"

Ned had gained some level of trust in himself and his new friends. "Maybe. But if I get scared, you have to help me back to the shore."

"It's a deal!"

Alexh loved feeling in control of the situation. She was hoping that all of her effort might get them to the other side quickly. She walked out till the water reached her waist. She was feeling grateful for the sun finally warming the air around her. "Come on Ned. Just make it to me. It's not very deep here."

"How am I supposed to swim in this shallow water?"

"You don't have to swim right away. You only have to make it as far as you trust. Try running in the water."

The water carried the majority of Ned's weight. He was able to move fast. He gradually ran in deeper water and found confidence in how the water carried his body.

"Hey you're doing great! Now come back and get me!"

Ned tried to swim by Alexh, but she grabbed his fur and pulled herself on top. Most of Ned's body remained just below the surface. He wasn't so sure about carrying the additional weight, but found he could barely feel the little gnome. Povh waded out to Ned and climbed aboard as well."

"Hey, I didn't agree to this!"

"Come on Ned. I bet you can do this in deeper water too. I bet you could make it across the lake in no time at all."

Ned swam quickly across the lake. Alexh and Povh were giggling and cheering as they rode Ned to the other side. Alexh had not realized how she had come to depend on Ned as much as he depended on her. He had saved the day more than once now. He did this just by being himself.

They decided to stop for a rest on a large warm stone shore. It

was sleek and dark. The collection of large flat stones drew a lot of heat from the sun. The berries were only a short distance away now. The warm sun felt so good against both skin and fur. They laid out flat on their backs and took a nap as they gradually dried.

When Alexh awoke she began to watch the trees move with the breeze. She wondered how their messages reach Ned. She held her eyes closed again and tried very hard to hear a tree voice. She couldn't even imagine what a tree voice must sound like. Then she noticed Ned lying awake staring at the trees as well. "Ned, I wonder what the trees talk about when they are talking to each other?"

Ned rolled over to Alexh, "Do you want me to tell you?"

Alexh smiled as she enjoyed the sun hitting her face, "Of course I do."

"They are very proud of you because you have learned so much."

"But I still haven't learned anything yet."

"They said that you have learned to be the student and the teacher at the same time. They also say that you will need that for the rest of your journey."

"Then if I have already learned this, where is Minx? Why hasn't she retuned?"

"Oh no! They say she still cannot return, but our time together is nearly over."

"Why?"

Ned began making a clicking noise.

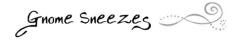

"Ned, where is Minx?"

The clicking noise continued and Alexh asked Povh, "What is wrong with Ned?"

Povh responded with squeaking and high pitch purring. The spell had worn off, and Alexh would need to rely on the relationship they had built. She can no longer understand their every sound.

Chapter 6
Beautiful

Alexh was very disappointed to see the magick spell that gave her so much insight had disappeared. "I suppose if I still needed it, it would still be here, right guys?"

Povh began to lick Alexh's face and Ned nearly sat on her. He sometimes forgets how big he is.

Alexh stood up in her warm dry cloths. She just realized that hunger returned. "Come on guys, let's get those berries!"

Alexh, Povh and Ned headed toward the prized berry bushes. Povh and Ned suddenly stopped. They began nervously looking around in all directions. Ned romped right back into the water but Povh would not leave Alexh's side. He began tugging at her cloths and barking and growling. Alexh was not listening to the way they were communicating with her. She was allowing herself to get frustrated with their behavior. "We've almost made it Povh! What is wrong with you!" Alexh sneezed, "Ishu, ishu!"

Just then Povh appeared larger. Alexh could not pull away from him. He grew to twice the size he was previously and

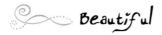

was able to drag her back into the water. Alexh became angry with him. The more she resisted the more he became a bigger obstacle.

Alexh sat in the water, sopping wet, staring at the berries she wanted so much. She became so slippery that Povh had a difficult time holding onto her, without accidentally scratching her up. She continued to try to get to shore, but Povh continued to pull her back. She wondered who's magick was causing Povh to be so much bigger and stronger. Just as her hand finally touched the shore again a Fachan was suddenly awakened. He slowly crawled out from under the bushes. Alexh was terrified and wishing she had listened to Ned and Povh.

The Fachan enjoyed stepping gradually closer to Alexh as he watched her standing frozen with fear. Then he noticed Ned. A purely malicious toothy grin crept across his bristly face as he saw the platypus. He stepped to the water's edge contemplating his revenge upon the creature that caused him so much pain the night before. He thought that all was within his grasp until he caught a glimpse of trouble in the corner of his eye.

A large green goblin suddenly jumped out into the clearing. "Blah-blah blblblbl! Plplpl!"

This Fachan had tangled with goblins before and found it not worth the risk. He swiftly disappeared into the berry bushes where he came from. Another goblin appeared behind. The little explorers were now surrounded. The sun glistened against the leathery green wrinkled skin of the first goblin. He puffed himself up with outrage as he approached and flashed a fierce look at Alexh. "Were you not told that this side of the lake is dangerous?"

Alexh shrugged her shoulders and took a step back.

His arms began to swing in all directions as he became more animated over his outrage and exclaimed, "Hmm, let's see you were told from the other side of the lake, not to come here, then your friends told you to get away quickly and yet you chose not to listen, right?"

Alexh didn't have an answer for him. She was caught between feeling ashamed and afraid.

"Oh, and did you enjoy the Fachan? You must have enjoyed the Fachan. There was nothing anyone could do to help you avoid him."

"No. I didn't enjoy him. He's a bad creature?"

"Oh, and judging too? You're batting zero here."

"What?"

"You heard me! You are judging him for protecting his own territory."

"What about him coming after us in the tree?"

"He's a teacher like any other. His true weapon is fear. He cannot harm you if you've learned to overcome fear. He's a great teacher! He also teaches awareness"

"He's wise?"

The large goblin stopped to scratch his chin and said, "Well no. He's not terribly bright, but that makes no less a teacher...."

The softer looking grayish goblin emerged from the brush interrupting, "And you're not terribly polite are you! Be nice to the little gnome. You have given her credit for nothing."

She smiled at Alexh and then glanced at Ned and Povh. "It is time that everyone returned from where they came." She patted Ned on the beak and said, "You, little friend do not belong in this land at all. You're mother waits for you in a land far away from here. You should say goodbye now."

He sensed that she was comforting and safe. He rubbed his beak against Alexh's face and then allowed the goblin to take him away into the forest.

"Where is she taking Ned", Alexh asked, alarmed by seeing her friend taken.

"Home. He is going home to his family. There are no others here like him. It is a good time to take you home as well."

"But I'm not ready to go home. I want to see Minx again."

The goblin ignored Alexh's protest. "There is another here. Polvindr! Where are you?"

The young Ghillie dhu stepped out into the opening. He stared at the ground looking sheepish. "Just Vindr. They call me Vindr."

"You know how much trouble you have caused?" puffed the angry goblin. "Hmf!"

"I know I'm in trouble."

"Hmf, thinking of yourself. Have you thought about your family or Minx? It is time for you to return."

Vindr got scared, because he too was not ready to go home. He ran back into the bushes as the angry goblin just grumbled at him.

Alexh was worried as she looked into the goblins deep black eyes lacking any sign of where the pupil began and where the white part normally is with speaking creatures. She wanted to be with Minx and hoped that this creature could just leave her with a familiar face. "What about Minx? What has happened? What does the Gillie Dhu have to do with anything?"

"Hmf. There are many rumors in the forest. There is time to discuss this later. If you are not ready to go home then you must go with me."

Alexh clung to Povh. She did not like the idea of going anywhere with this creature. "What if I don't want to?"

"You don't get a choice. We need to figure out what to do with you now." The goblin paused, shook his head and took a deep breath. "I apologize for my rudeness. There is a lot to correct now. My name is Renart and my wife, who you've met briefly is Raimunde. It is not safe to just leave you here. If you'd like to be helpful in retrieving your friend you must follow me."

71

Alexh was very frightened, but followed Renart into the forest. Within a few minutes they arrived at a tree that was completely bent over into an arch. "What a strange way for a tree to grow." She whispered to Povh.

"This is a faerie door. It is the way back to the world most faerie folkies live. Your people chose to forget how to return, which is why you don't know about them." Renart informed Alexh as he nudged her through the door.

As they walked through, the scenery mutated into a completely different place. It was like a cave but huge and well lit from the circular tunnels above that went straight out to the light. There were stalactites and stalagmites as well as the roots of trees in some places. The floor was stone and some areas looked as if someone had purposely crafted and fitted decorative stone together to create an interesting look.

There were tables with food, music playing and goblins

dancing, running and swinging everywhere.

A large old hairy goblin approached Alexh and patted her on the back as he exclaimed, "Ah, you've arrived in time for dinner!"

Alexh thought that was odd, since it was only lunch time in the world she came from. She looked around and continued to cling tightly to Povh. "Povh, here's the plan; you get their attention while I dash back through..."

Before she could finish her sentence, Povh had torn away and began to romp around with the young goblins. Alexh remembered that Povh's pretty good at knowing what's going on, so if he thinks this is a good place to play and have fun, then it must be safe.

Alexh approached a large table full of food she loved and other foods she found unrecognizable. She reached for an apple, but it was snatched away by a young goblin before she could get to it. Two other little goblins played chase around her and then ran away. She began to feel exhausted just looking around.

"Is it always like this, Renart?"

"At dinner time"

"I'm used to something more organized."

Renart smiled at Alexh as he nudged her with his elbow. "That's okay you'll blend in, in no time." Winking at her he walked away to greet other goblins.

Alexh felt confused. She meant to say that this was a little to rowdy for her, but Renart seemed to be excusing her for not fitting in.

Beautiful

She sat down on a bench wedged between a rocky wall and a row of tables. Before her hungry eyes was the amazing spread of foods with variation into infinity. She passed over all of the most exotic looking dishes and began to snack on bread with honey butter. As she found the bread to be the most aromatic and softest bread she had ever tasted. She feasted on baked apples and rice with spicy carrot sauce. Although there were lots of other foods, these were the foods she was used to. She began to calm down and watch the excitement quietly. Povh had been racing around letting the goblins toss food into his mouth. She was taken aback with how different each goblin appeared. Their eyes were of varied colors that mimicked the bright sheen of polished semi-precious stones. Renart's eyes reminded her of obsidian. Raimonde had eyes like Lapis. It was good to see that she too had arrived in time for dinner.

The colors of their eyes were not uniform and did not form a circular design. Some were also very striking like gold and silver or flecks of either. Their ears and noses came in endless sizes and shapes. She couldn't stop staring at them all. She had never seen so much variation in a singe species. They were also the most entertaining folkies she had met yet. They pulled each others ears, and played practical jokes and tickled and even tossed one another around the room. She was surprised that no one seemed at all upset. In fact, the victim

74

of every prank laughed and chased after their prankster with glee.

Alexh looked toward Renart. He had a deep full bodied laugh, similar to that of her father. He was stern, yet kind and gentle. He unknowingly made Alexh feel at home. "Renart, why aren't they getting mad when the other goblins play tricks on them?"

Renart laughed, "Don't you enjoy a good joke?"

"No."

"What about all of the time and thought that goes into figuring out just the right way to trick you?" squinting those weird eyes as he smirked.

"No"

"Hmf, then you haven't really thought about it. Your friend Minx goes to great lengths to get me soaked anytime she can. I, in return set traps to get her wet, muddy or otherwise compromised. We are good friends!"

"Look, I know when other gnomes play tricks on me, it's because they DON'T like me." Alexh said with a tiny squeak at the end and trying to control her bottom lip that quivered slightly.

"Why wouldn't they like you?"

"Because I'm different. They like my sisters, but not me." Alexh began to sniffle and cry, "They're pretty. Ishu!" Alexh's hair began to turn moss green and became the texture of hay.

Renart stroked her hair and turned it back before the change was noticeable to Alexh. "Oh, Alexh, you don't understand

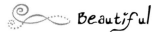 Beautiful

what beauty is. You've been
staring at us for a while. Are we
still so ugly to you?"

"No, not really. I wouldn't mind
staying here. Everyone likes
each other."

"But do you see their beauty?"

"What do you mean?"
Renart took Alexh by the hand
and lead her outside to a tropical
garden. As far as she could see
there were amazing colorful
plants in endless variety.

"Alexh, which ones are the
prettiest?"

"I don't know. Maybe that
one, that one, that one..." she
continued to point to the infinite
assortment.

"Why do you think they are the
very best ones?"

"Because, I've never seen anything like them before."

"Ah, so it's the differences that catch your eyes! That's
how we see each other. We have a strong appreciation for
variation. Ah, my Raimonde. I love her long droopy ears, her
curled up nose and her funny smile. Oh, she can make me
laugh so easily when she makes faces at me. I love her so."

A few young goblins began to run out to the garden. Alexh

watched the goblins play, swinging from vines and being silly. They had a sort of woven stretchy vine with a strange hook on one end. A goblin would hook it into the high branches and let themselves drop and bounce back up. They have the ability to move great distances quickly in a heavily wooded forest. It was impressive to see them zip all over with the aid of these tools, and their great strength and agility.

"Yeah, they are very beautiful." Alexh smiled and waved at them.

"And what about you?"

"No. I don't see that at all." She looked down sadly.

Renart took her to the edge of a peculiar fountain. There were a dozen strange faces carved into the stone with water pouring out of nostrils mouths or ears. The pool below it had colorful fish swimming contently. As they approached the fish swam away into a cavern leaving the pool still and lifeless. "Look at your reflection Alexh."

"Yeah"

"I see spunky freckles, silky hair, big pretty eyes and a tiny nose. Excellent gnome qualities."

"But I'm a little chubbier than everyone else and my teeth are crooked!"

"Oh, I love crooked teeth! wish you'd flash me big crooked smile!"

I
a

77

 Beautiful

Alexh remained silent.

"And look at those long
lovely fingers! You should
play an instrument."

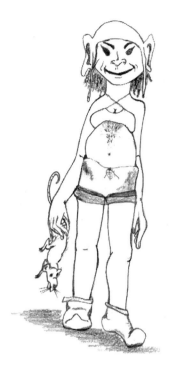

Alexh nodded, "Mamma
says that, sniff."

"Oh, Mamma is right. And
there are so many things
you do not yet know about
yourself. You are really
special and I would be
terribly disappointed if
you looked like every other
gnome.

Alexh threw her arms
around Renart and wept.

"And great hugs too. You're
magnificent."

"Can I stay here?"

"No. We're only one part of your journey. You'll have to go
home, but you are always welcome here."

Alexh slouched down and wiped her face.

"You see little gnome, your kind has long forgotten it's eternal
and etheric nature. You will cross the paths of all folkie in this
lifetime. You will experience their wisdom and know a deeper
magick. You have already learned more than you realize.

"I was supposed to learn how to talk to trees from Ned, and I didn't learn it."

"No, you were supposed to learn to listen to Ned and Povh, and you did learn it. You are learning to always be the teacher and the student. You have learned to listen to others around you, though you need practice." He said with a smile and a wink and then continued, "There is always value in this. One of your greatest gifts will be to appreciate the magick around you."

"How is that a gift?"
"You will see. Not all are able to appreciate the magick. For a gnome, you have been quite accepting of the magick of this world.

"I've heard this place is very dangerous."

"The dangers here are only different from those in your world. Just continue to listen. You don't have to always agree, but you have to listen. This puts you in a place of understanding and peace with anyone who is in conflict with you." Renart smiled peacefully at Alexh and turned down a path into the woods. Alexh wasn't clear on the meaning of everything Renart said to her, but decided that listening has become a common theme. In the past it hadn't occurred to her that listening and agreeing were not the same thing. Sometimes having respect for a very different set of values can be really hard.

Alexh noticed that many more goblins had left the dining hall. Some were running through the wooded play area with Povh. The youngest goblins seemed to be rolling around with him the most. It's a good thing he's so much bigger now and can take the rough and tumble playfulness of the goblin folkie. Some goblins had great prehensile tails to assist them in their acrobatic play in the trees. It was amazing to see them flip and turn and catch each other in the air. Some also juggled things and tossed objects back and forth to each other. They seemed

 Beautiful

to be very accurate in their tricks, but Alexh did not want to get hit by flying fruit or flying goblins, so she walked back towards the dining hall. She peered in and saw two larger goblins leading the dinner cleanup. They were managing two very large creatures with long snoots and long tongues. These animals were eating all of the leftovers and sucking up all the spills and licking every inch of the hall. Alexh shivered all over. She wondered a minute about the food preparation, but then decided it's probably best not to think about that.

When Alexh turned around, Raimonde was standing beside her holding two of the strange viney cords she had seen earlier. She could see the decorative weaving that caused the tool to be so elastic.

"Alexh, this is a chuba. It is a good form of transportation for us, because we are light ethereal beings with great upper body strength. This one has been made a bit smaller for you, since you are so much smaller than we goblins."

Alexh accepted the chuba, "Thank you, but I don't think I can do this."

"Oh, that is too bad, since your room is up there." Raimonde pointed high above the dining hall doorway, straight up a tall rock wall. The wall was covered in trees growing out of every crevice. Between the trees were decorative circular entryways. There were a few goblins using their chubas to quickly scale up the rock wall. They simply threw the end with the hook way up high, where it caught the branch of a tree. The force of the elasticity immediately pulled them up to the branch, where the hook was waiting to be thrown again.

"Isn't there another way?"

"No. This is the way. You can follow me to your room." Raimonde informed her as she flung her chuba and was ten

80

feet above Alexh in an instant.

Alexh flung the chuba at a branch and missed. She thought
about riding Povh up, but she didn't want to appear to be a
quitter. She continued to try and the hook finally caught a
branch, but the spring action was not enough to carry her up.
As a gnome, Alexh should have more control over her center
of gravity by now.   This is what gives the gnomes the ability
to run faster than any land animal and to be carried so easily
by birds and small mammals.

"Now what? The cord is not bringing me up."

Raimonde jumped to the branch where Alexh's hook was
caught. She released the hook and let it fall back to the ground.
"Try again Alexh, but this time concentrate on what it feels
like to glide through the air on Povh. You must remember
your etheric body. Focus with your third eye."

Alexh furrowed her brow at Raimonde, "Hey, I don't have a
third eye!"

A younger goblin responded as he rubbed his nose all the way
up to his forehead, "Maybe she can't see through it cause she
has boogers on it!"

"No I don't!"

Raimonde hushed the laughing, "Focus! You need to connect
yourself with the air element. The wind is how we recognize
its movement. Feel the air element moving through you. Try
singing to the wind. It will certainly answer a song from the
heart."

Alexh began to make half hearted humming sounds. She
continued to hum as she remembered Papa telling her to be
light as a gecko. "Raimonde, why is the gecko so light?"
The gecko knows the ancient magick of reversed gravity.

They use this magick with electromagnetic and electrostatic attraction. It is used to be drawn to the gravitational force of objects other than the ground. You too can claim this magick and the etheric nature your kind has forgotten. It exists in both worlds."

"How?"

"Focus Alexh. You are as much the air around you as you are your left big toe."

Alexh closed her eyes and imagined being the air. She began to bounce at her knees as if to mock the movement of being tossed in the wind. Then she started to hum what she believed the wind would hum like. Young goblins joined her in humming and began to imagine Alexh being part of the wind.

When Alexh could clearly see herself in the flow, moving up the wall, she began to sing,

> *Swing and sway, blow my way*
> *Flowing through me for today*
> *Flitter flutter air around*
> *Nothern southern whistle sound*
> *One with me, happily, lifting me off the ground*
> *Lifting, sifting flow with ease*
> *Like butterfly and buzzing bees*
> *Light as gecko on one toe*
> *Air within me, ground far below*

Alexh was suddenly filled with the confidence of an unwavering storm. She threw the chuba. It caught and carried her only a few feet up into the root system of another tree. She was elated to have moved at all. "Yay for me, the wind!" Raimonde again released the hook and Alexh began to imagine being the wind again. Though not as quickly as the goblins, she gradually made it up the mountain and to her

room. The journey up the wall was so much fun, it was a little disappointing to see her lesson come to an end. She turned and peered over the edge seeing Povh far below her, still playing with the youngest goblins.

In the instant she looked at him, Povh turned and saw Alexh had finally made it to the top. He scurried like lightning straight up through the winding trees and gnarly roots. Alexh was thrilled to have Povh pounce on her. "Hey there Povh." She cuddled with him for a moment and then gave her attention back to Raimonde, who was patiently waiting. Raimonde pulled a pair of goblin stretchy jammies out of her pouch. "You can shower and change into these. Leave your soiled cloths on a branch outside of your room. They will be clean for you in the morning." Then she turned and walked to the edge and literally dropped from sight.

Alexh was relieved to finally feel clean again after all they had been through. She chased Povh around the shower room and made sure he was clean head to toe. After dressing for bed they romped around the room from one hammock to the next. Vines seemed to be the main furniture staple for goblins. There were hammocks, hanging chairs, hanging table, hanging gourd planters even hanging contraptions to put your stuff if you had anything.

Alexh could have put her new chuba there if she hadn't already thrown it on the floor right next to her dirty cloths that were supposed to go outside. She admired the beautiful macramé wall hangings that boasted the only real color in the room. Everything else mostly remained in their natural colors. The goblins had a special way of weaving the vines so that they stretched. The hanging chairs were the most comfortable chairs she had ever sat in, despite being made for folkies at least four times her size. Every bit of décor was completely different from the articulately carved furniture her father made and her mother painted with brightly colored natural

dyes. This furniture was also more tolerant of all the jumping swinging and bouncing Alexh and Povh had inflicted. In time the two settled down and slept together comfortably on a nice big hammock.

That night Alexh had a terrible nightmare. She found herself alone with no one to protect her. Povh was small enough to be carried around. He was not in any position to help her anymore.

They were lost in the forest somewhere in the faerie world and Alexh was trying to get herself and Povh out safely. She began to hear scary noises, followed by scary eyes, followed by being chased by huge scary creatures! Everywhere she turned, danger found them.

She could see her home in the distance but the more she ran the further it seemed to get from her. Her ability to run was hampered by some magickal force. Then her slow motion was reduced to crawling as she saw her home disappear into the distance. Heavy vines appeared all over the path. She began to get completely tangled in them. She looked around for the tiny version of Povh but could not find him.

Alexh awoke alone, wrapped in the vine hammock. She released her grip on the hammock and fell to the cold hard floor. She walked out to the ledge. Povh had returned to his original size. He was laying down sunning himself as he peered peacefully down into the forest. "Hey there Povh." She snuggled up to him and watched him continue to stare into the forest. He looked a little sad. "I know boy, you probably miss home as much as I do." He gave a brief squeak confirming her assertion.

The sounds of playing and the smell of food wafted up the side of the mountain to Povh and Alexh. Povh began to get a little more lively. Alexh noticed her clean cloths hanging on a branch, just outside of their room. She changed quickly, grabbed her chuba and the two quickly glided down to the breakfast chaos.

Tables were setup outside that were covered in fruit, rice granola and other foods that were completely unidentifiable to Alexh. Some goblins actually grabbed food from the table as they swung by on vines. Another hung upside-down at the table from a vine with the assistance of his fancy prehensile tail. There were older goblins weaving clothing, hangings, furniture and tools. Younger goblins were taking lessons as they snacked from the table. Others gathered to head to the gardens. There was no division by age or gender. Anyone could weave, anyone could garden or do anything else they felt like doing. It was as if what Alexh considered a chore, goblins considered part of the fun.

Alexh sat down at the table on a bench next to Renart. She began to tell him about her dream and asked him to tell her what he thought about it. She remembered that Minx said that dreams are great teachers.

"Perhaps your dream is only telling you that your fears and your dependence on Povh are the only things that are keeping your from attaining your peace."

"How am I dependent on Povh?"

"It is good that Povh is also becoming your friend. I know you loved him before, but now your relationship has changed. He has taught you a lot about your own impulsivity. You trust his instinct and his knowledge of terrain. Do not fear the day you can no longer ride. By that time, you will not need him for transportation. What you will need is the lessons he teaches you now"

"But it feels wonderful to glide through the air. There is

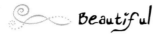

nothing else like it."

"True, but you will value your new skills and future adventures as much as you do this youthful gliding time in your life."

"I'm so glad coming here has been part of my adventure. Now I know what goblins are like."

"Hahaha! Is that what you think? You think you have found variation of kind here. Just wait till you see the rest of our world."

"Are some dangerous?"

"Oh yes."

Alexh grimaced in fear.

"But I hope you never run out of new experiences with every kind of goblin and every kind of other folkie here."

"How many kinds are there?"

Just then Alexh noticed a viney little hand reaching out and stealing food from the table. Renart looked over to see what Alexh was looking at. He smiled and walked into the heavy brush just behind them. Suddenly Renart jumped back out of the brush right where the viney hand was. He was holding Vindr!

"Ah ha! So now you are ready to repair the damage you have done, yes?"

"Is Minx really in trouble? Asked the spindly young gillie with worry and tears in his eyes.

"Yes, I believe she truly is in trouble. Otherwise, she would have appeared by now.

"Where is she?"

"In a cage of iron, waiting to appear before Gillie Dhu trial."

"Why?" the two youngsters asked.

"Oh, a number of things. The king is completely fed up with her interference in the forest. He believes her actions are against the nature of the forest. He also believes his son disappeared with a gnome and Minx."

Vindr hung his head in shame.

"Vindr, I don't care whether or not you stay there, but you must take Alexh and Povh to the birch forest. It is her destiny to defend Minx."

"What? What would I say?" piped Alexh.

"You will use everything you have learned so far in this land. You will remember all that she has taught you and remember what is right and wrong in the eyes of the forest."

"But I don't know enough to help." Alexh puffed with doubt.

"And as for you, adventuresome gillie; you have made it your destiny to ensure Alexh's success. When you avoid your lessons, you realize they keep track of you, correct?"

"I know. I will take them."

"Ah, then we are nearly ready. Alexh, Raimonde will of course prepare you for your trip. Vindr and I will have a talk."

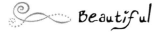 Beautiful

Raimonde spent time training Alexh on her chuba. She told her that she may need to use this skill on her journey. Alexh didn't understand the importance of this skill since she had Povh to carry her anywhere she needed to go.

"Raimonde, I don't see how this is going to help me. I don't feel ready to rescue Minx. I'm so little and I have very little magick." She said as she stared at the ground moving dirt around with her toes."

"Ah, little gnome. Have you not learned that you are as much the forest as I am, as the Gillie Dhu are and as much as your friend Minx? Are you not learning to have more confidence in yourself as you learn your center of balance? And have you not learned that the forest knows when you are ready for the next lesson?"

Alexh felt like that was too many questions at once. "I don't know. You're confusing me! I just don't understand how what I know can help anyone else."

"Alexh, you must trust that Renart and I can see that you have exactly what is needed to understand the Gillie Dhu king. You are the epitome of everything he is missing at this point in time. I trust that you will simply express your knowledge and do what is in your heart. Do you trust in our judgment?"

"I suppose…"

"Ah, then it is done." Raimonde threw up her arms and began gathering odd fruits from a basket on the table that everyone eats breakfast from. She tucked the snacks into the hip satchel that was made especially for Alexh.

Alexh soon met up with Vindr again, but didn't get to hear whatever he and Renart had discussed. Just knowing that they had a discussion gave Alexh little more confidence in this

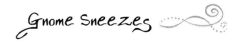

elusive Gillie Dhu.

"So, you know the way?" Alexh asked in a friendly manner. "Of course I know the way. I'm a Gillie Dhu. The forest speaks to me and heeds my command."

Alexh furrowed her brow at him. She didn't like feeling so ordinary.

Renart took Alexh's hand, "I love how you are always so eager to trust the forest. The forest holds so many surprises for you and I know that you welcome the unexpected now." He then glanced back at Vindr and added, "And hopefully all will learn from Alexh's grand bravery."

CHAPTER 7

Vindr's arms grew out into long vines which he used to swing through the trees like a monkey. Alexh and Povh glided behind him. Povh really wanted to catch Vindr, so he was enjoying the chase as Vindr purposely zipped back and forth between the trees.

Gliding over the vast green forest Alexh spotted a large dark wall ahead. Alexh became curious and veered Povh toward the wall. As they approached she could see tall flowering trees peeking out over the top. Vindr looked back and saw Alexh heading slightly off course. He doubled back to get them back on track but then noticed where they were headed. He lingered with distance between them and yelled out upon the wind, "Hey you! You're going the wrong way!" Disgruntled he whispered to himself, "Stupid gnome." As much as Vindr enjoyed treating Alexh to magickal gifts unseen, he felt some

jealousy towards her. He resented the favoritism Renart showed her when he complimented her bravery. Suddenly Alexh felt more like an annoying little sister who couldn't keep in step.

Alexh looked back in the direction the wind carried Vindr's voice from. "I just want to get a quick look over the wall." she said, hoping Vindr could hear.

Vindr again attempted to capture Alexh's attention, "Steer clear of it!"

Alexh had been walking along a branch that ran against the top of the wall. She began to wonder if this place could be dangerous. Povh had run ahead of her and had already scampered across the wall. "Povh, no, get back here! We should go!"

It was too late. Something had caught his attention. He leaped from sight leaving Alexh in shock.

"Povh!" Alexh ran to the wall and looked down, expecting to catch him getting into something he shouldn't be messing with. To her surprise, Povh was nowhere to be seen. "Povh? Povh! Where are you?"

Vindr smacked himself in the head and then tucked himself away into the greenery to wait until their return.

Alexh felt very leery of this garden. She used her chuba to lower herself to the ground and continued to call out to Povh. She sporadically looked back hoping to see Vindr, but he too was out of sight. She was alone in the garden hoping to find Povh quickly and be on her way to Minx.

As she wandered deeper into the garden she realized that there was something very odd about the silence there. She

heard no living thing. All she heard was the cascading sounds of a fountain in the distance and the rustling of the trees around her. "Where are the birds?" she whispered to herself.

A well crafted little cobb home was visible just beyond the fountain. The trees and flowers were unnaturally perfect, and again she could see fruits like she had never seen in the world she came from. "Are there goblins here?"

The door to the house was slightly ajar, and just enough for her to peek inside. The home was simple and kept neat. There was a large counter with fancy aromatic fruits in a bowl. The cabinets were an ornate reminder of her parents home. In fact the hominess of the entire house reminded her of being at home, with the exception of the larger size. She crept into the house and whispered, "Povh, are you in here? Come out."

She approached a big beautiful fireplace. As she walked past a

chair that was facing the fireplace the folkie sitting in it cleared his throat, making his presence known.

"Eek!" Alexh jumped back. "Um sorry? Looking for my pet?"

"I see you have familiarized yourself with my home."

"I didn't mean to… Well I didn't see.."

"No worries gnome. I suppose yeh have a name?"

Alexh took a step back and quietly responded, "Alexh."

"Alexh, and odd name for a gnome. Haven't heard that one before."

"Do you know other gnomes?"

"I'm a very old folkie. I've met many other folkie in meh time."

"Well my friend is missing."

"I thought yeh said pet?"

"Well, yes. He's both you see."

"Hmmm, haven't seen anyone else wanderin around meh home. Just you. Perhaps you'll have a bit o tea with meh? I do have a very good mint tea that gnomes are particularly fond of."

Alexh's eyes grew large, "Mint tea?"

As the tall folkie stood up he towered over Alexh. He was at least five feet tall, which was taller than any folkie she'd ever seen before. He stepped closer to her and bent down towards her with a toothy grin and said, "Oh yes, and I believe there are some tender acorn biscuits in the cupboard. Does that interest yeh as well?"

Alexh stepped back again.

"You needn't be worried gnome. If I wanted to eat yeh, you'd be gone by now."

Alexh furrowed her brow at him, "You eat gnomes?"

"Beggin your pardon mam, but if I did, you wouldn't make much of a meal, now would yeh."

Alexh ignored his boldness as she brushed her hair over to one

side and told him, "I really need to find my friend and be on my way."

"Well, then! We'll be taken the tea on the road. Let's have a walkabout the garden, shall we? You me and a cup o' tea meh lady."

The strange folkie danced a bit as he took a pot of tea from the stove and filled two cups. One was just small enough for Alexh to handle. Alexh then followed the folkie back outside where it was still unnaturally quiet.

"So, what were you an yer little friend doing all the way out here? This is a long way from where any gnome lives. I didn't know of any gnomes venturin into this world anymore."

"I'm here to help my friend Minx."

"Minx yeh say? Haven't seen her in bit."

"You know Minx?" Alexh's eyes lit up. She began to loosen up and enjoy sipping her tea.
"Oh, I know many many folkies of this world. There are few that are unknown to meh. You are the mystery I'm curious aboot today."

"Me? A mystery?"

"Don't think so lightly of yourself deary. Little bitty gnome like you, all alone in a big magickal world here. You must have some hidden power?"

"I don't know what my magick is yet."

"Yeh don't say? Well, perhaps you'd like to learn some magick? You'd be going home with wisdom the other gnomes don't have."

"I don't know. What kind of magick?"

"I know a lot of magick. Could teach yeh anything you'd like. My gifts are grand and the price is small."

"What is the price?"
"Just yer friendship my dear. Can you promise meh that?"

"My friendship? I don't understand. That's not so valuable? Why do you want it? My friendship that is."

"I find it very valuable. Friends trust each other, correct?"

"Yes."

"Friends help one another, correct?"

"Yeah."

"And friends keep their promises, correct?"

"Sure. I can keep a promise. What will you teach me?"

"Are you promising yer friendship to meh?"

Alexh felt a lump in the pit of her stomach. It seemed like a simple request that couldn't possibly do any harm. "Yeah, sure. I promise to be your friend."

"And you promise never to retract this friendship?"

"Yes. I wouldn't do that. I can be your friend."

"Oh, what a delight! What gifts I have for Alexh, meh new friend."

"I need something that will help me with the Gillie Dhu king."

"Ah, so you're going to see old knot-head himself are yeh?"

"He has captured my friend Minx, and I'm going to get her back."

"You're a brave one, for a gnome. How were you planning to do that?"

"I think I'm supposed to speak on her behalf. I have to convince him to let her go."

"And what were yeh planning to do if the old knot-head's too full of himself to listen to a fine young gnome like yerelf? He can be quite cantankerous yeh know."

Alexh took on Minx's mischievous smile for a moment as she delightfully announced, "Then I'll zap him with magick and make him listen to me!"

"Ah, I was hoping you'd make such a suggestion. I've just the magick for yeh." The odd elfish character reached into his pocket and held something tight between his index finger and thumb. "We shall only need a pinch of this."

He dropped the tiny grains into the hollow of a tulip and then whistled over it. A bit of dew immediately dissolved the grains so that they were no longer visible. Soon a butterfly came to the tulip and sipped away every drop of the potion.

"Doesn't look all that magickal to me."

"Give it a moment, meh friend."

The butterfly flittered about Alexh's head. It appeared to

be growing each time it passed before her eyes. Gracefully it flittered straight up as it grew to more than ten times its original size. Then the giant butterfly darted back towards Alexh. Alexh began to run as fast as she could. Its long dangly tongue brushed at her making a loud slurping sound.

"No! Help! Make it stop!"

The odd little character began to laugh with a loud cackle. Alexh became terrified as it seemed she would soon become food for the giant butterfly. "No! Get away from me!" She swung her arms at the long rubbery hose like tongue and then, "Ishu!"

The giant butterfly disappeared. Alexh looked around and then saw the tiny butterfly fluttering around her again. "Stupid butterfly." Then she noticed that the entire garden looked different. It was not as lush as it was a moment before. There were far fewer fruit on the trees and the fountain barely trickled. There were vines that covered the imperfect paths through the garden. "What just happened?"

"You ruined the illusion." Said the old hunched over figure that walked toward her.

"You're a Fir Darrig?"

"Yes, I am. Does it bother yeh?" said the now, old and gruesome being standing before her.

"Well, aren't you dangerous?"

"Not to meh friends." He said quietly as he straightened his frumpled cloths.

Alexh suddenly remembered her promise. Then she heard a squeaking sound. She looked in all directions and began

to run through the trees. Finally she saw what she had been looking for. "Povh!"

Her glider was running towards her and squeaking loudly.

"Where have you been? Why didn't you come to me sooner?"

The Fir Darrig caught up to Alexh and calmly approached her. "He has been distracted meh dear." The Fir Darrig waved his hand at Povh. The glider suddenly lost interest in Alexh and started jumping around, as if he was trying to catch something.

"What is he doing? What have you done to my friend?"

"A friend of yours is indeed a friend of mine. Povh is a bit distracted for now. He believes he is jumping at and enjoying something he likes best."

"Probably grasshoppers. Why have you trapped him? Please let him go. He means everything to me. Please let me have him back." Alexh pleaded.

"I have every intension of given em back. I only caught em to bring yeh here. I have a favor to ask of yeh. In return, I will release your friend. I'll also help yeh wit ol splinter britches."

"Who?"

"The Gillie Dhu king. I can help yeh, if only you'd be letting meh. I'll give yeh what's needed to overcome the king. You'll be need'n to learn a few things from me, an then you'll be set."

"Why should I trust you?"

"I'm a friend. Yeh may not understand meh humor and meh ways. Yeh may not even like meh very much, but yeh needn't worry aboot have'n a friend in meh."

"The only power you have is illusion. What good is that to me?"

"Why, illusion's a powerful tool. Just look it how yeh reacted to meh butterfly illusion."

"Yeah, cause you were gonna let that giant butterfly eat me!"

"Now, don't yeh be blaming meh for where you took that illusion."

"Me!"

"An illusion's only what yeh make of it. I can create the illusion to allow you to distract yourself or I can choose to teach you something with it. It's meh choice. But you should be knowin that the illusion needs yer hopes and fears to take action en to take form. Do yeh think the illusion could eat yeh?"

"I don't know. Everything changed before it could eat me."

"Is that what you'd be thinkin? Hahahaha! Well I have a bit of a surprise for yeh. Yer one powerful magickal gnome. If yeh ever get control o that magick, I'd be interested in seeing what yeh do wit it."

"What do you mean?"

"Somethin tells meh it's nah time for yeh to know yer magick just yet. But I promise yeh, yer gonna be a real handful to ol splinter britches!" He laughed and choked and laughed some more.

Alexh didn't know what to think of so much laughter

and happiness coming from this gruesome character. She
furrowed her brow at him and began to ask, "So what's my
magi..."

"Oh no, you won't be gettin it out o meh darlin. Yeh know,
yeh may nah be needn meh help at all, but if'n yeh find yerself
in a jam, I want yeh to dump the mixture into the tub o water
he rests his feet in at night.

Alexh watched the fir darrig pull a scrappy looking little
bag out of his pocket and hand it to her. She opened it and
examined the sandy mixture inside. She looked at the fir
darrig and asked, "What will this do?"

"Oh now, you needn't be worrin yerself boot these things
lassie. I promise yeh that there will be no permanent damage
done. Yeh said it yerself, meh only magick is illusion. Yeh
don't believe that an illusion is powerful magick, so it
shouldn't be botherin yeh to use the magick."

"But what will it do?"

"That there depends on ol splinter britches. I'll be watchin. I'll
be letting yer friend go the minute the mixture hits the water
darling."

"No! I can't do this without Povh! I need him. Please give him
back now!"

"Darlin, I know this seems cruel, but it's for yer own good; an
for the good o Povh. If yeh get yerself in the clink, yeh don't
want anything to happen to him do yeh?"

Alexh gazed at Povh still chasing the illusion. He was
completely unaware of her presence. "At least he looks
happy." she whispered to herself.

"Do you feel ready to face the king all on yer own, without my

help? I think yer a bit afraid, now aren't yeh?"

"Maybe."

"I'm just sayin deary, this magick can help you in a jam. Use it or not, I'll be releasing Povh the minute you overcome ol' splinter britches. Does that sound better to yeh? Do we have deal?"

Alexh nodded and silently walked back towards the wall. She casually looked back at Povh a few times and then climbed the wall. Once she was able to use her chuba to move through the first few trees, Vindr appeared.

"What have you done? Where is Povh?"

Alexh felt terribly ashamed of losing Povh. "He's safe. I don't want to talk about it anymore." She tried to convince herself that leaving him behind was for the best, although leaving him stuck in an illusion didn't seem to be her idea of safe. She simply had to put the whole matter out of her mind and focus on using her chuba to quickly get her to the birch forest.

Alexh gradually got better at using the chuba and Vindr had to stop less frequently to let her catch up.

CHAPTER 8
Nature of the Forest

When they arrived, they could see Minx and the iron cage she was being held in. Long iron spikes pierced the ground and curled up towards the top with a large viney knot. Minx did not even have the strength to stand. The iron poisoning had drained her of the strength to use her power.

"Why hasn't Minx disappeared to somewhere else?"

"You go back to your world, and this is her world." Vindr, continued, "My father had each piece of that cage brought into this world very carefully, specifically for the purpose of containing Minx. I've heard about her for a long time. She meddles with everyone, everything, everywhere. That's why I followed you. She looked so happy, and like she'd be so much fun. I knew it had to be her. I've always been curious about her. I was just waiting to get my courage up to announce myself, until she disappeared. I didn't know I'd cause this."

"Well you did! Now you have to help me."

"No way. He's really angry this time. Besides, it's all your destiny! You fix it and I'll catch up with you later."

"No! I don't know what..."

It was too late. Vindr had disappeared into the forest with no signs of his presence.

"I don't know what to do without you." She mumbled to herself as she glanced at the forest walls.

"Well, I'd better do something." Alexh said as she approached the cage. Gnomes are not allergic to iron, so she grabbed the iron and started to pull as hard as she could. She was hoping to pull the cage over and out of the ground. Just then she found herself completely surrounded by Gillie dhu. "Stop gnome!"

 Nature of the Forest

Minx finally looked up, "Alexh, what are you doing here?"

"I'm here to get you out of trouble?"

The king approached Alexh, "And how do you plan to get Minx out of trouble?"

"I will speak on her behalf. She is a good pixie."

"Hahahaha! She is nothing but trouble, meddling with all things natural. Her powers have been misused to cause all things unnatural. We put the kibosh on it right now. I see you are a naive little gnome and you think you know something about this dark dream I do not. You will be given the opportunity to speak your peace. We can begin now."

The other Gillie dhu brought out a nice chair for the king. He sat directly in front of Alexh and Minx. "Continue little gnome."

Alexh was nervous and unprepared. She looked at Minx, who seemed to be sleeping through her own trial. "I don't know where to begin, really. Minx has taught me a lot about myself and how to control my temper. She taught me that everyone is magickal and that everyone is both the student and the teacher."

"These are simple teachings. Did she teach you to take what is not yours and to pixie nap as well?"
"No. I got lost and your son didn't even let us know he was following us!"

"Nonsense, where is my son! What have you done with him?!"

Vindr had been watching silently. He was still not ready to come out.

Gnome Sneezes

"I saw him. The Goblins caught him, but then he got away!" She exclaimed as her face began to turn red.

"You are a liar! Goblins could never catch my Vindr. He is swift and undetectable."

"I'm not lying! He…ishu!" She sneezed and the kings chair turned into a pile of green beans.

The king was shocked, then turned to her with a look of resolution, "Who is your father?!"

"Papa?"

"His real name!"

Alexh was frightened and slowly stepped backwards until she bumped into more Gillie Dhu. She answered, "I've heard him called Odimar."

The king leaned back into the large pile of green beans, "I knew your father. He had the gnome allergy, as you are developing."

"I have an allergy? To what?"

The king arrogantly ignored her question and continued, "I remember your father as a young man. His allergy was terrible. Every time he got angry he would sneeze and upset all of nature. Trees fell down, rivers would run the wrong way, rain turned to butter and even the wind would refuse to carry our voice. We Gillie Dhu would rarely walk into the other world; only to avoid his presence. He was sent away from the gnome villages, because of his terrible disruption to their lives."

"My papa did all of that?"

"And more. Animals feared his presence. He lived deep in the forest completely alone.

Then one day a large bear noticed him. She watched how his peptflitter would flare and strange things would happen around him with every gnome sneeze. He was, as all gnomes, allergic to peptiflitter. The allergy can develop in teen years and generally is outgrown by most. Your father did not outgrow the allergy and by this time he was dangerous to all things. The bear enjoyed the sweet butter that came down around the strange gnome. She followed him everywhere he went. This would make him angry. He only wished to be alone. He tried to loose her, but there was no way. Crazy things like mushrooms turning blue and radishes growing from the trees would always give his location away."

"My papa hates radishes."

"Predictable. He could not create things to enjoy in this condition. The bear was crazy about him. There was nothing that could frighten her away, and he was not capable of creating anything that would frighten her. It was the forest taking care of itself.

Time went by and she wanted to help him. She did not know how to control his sneezes. When she saw him begin to sniffle, she sat on him immediately. Then he would be stuck under her and could barely breathe.
This bear was large and smelly. He did not like being stuck under her. When this would happen he would forget all that he was angry about and wait to be released. In time, the little things that would normally upset him, did not seem so bad. Nothing was as bad as being trapped under the buttocks of this bear. The upset to the forest seemed to die away and we never heard of him again after this. The forest itself obviously fixed the problem."

"That doesn't sound like my Papa."

"Perhaps you don't know what he's capable of."

Alexh felt deeply insulted and spouted, "You don't know my Papa. He's kind and gentle and doesn't have this allergy."

"Don't you tell me what I don't know. I have seen how dangerous he has been to the forest. Dangerous like you; against the will of the forest. You have not changed my mind. You have made my mind up. Lock her up!"

The Ghillie Dhu began to corner Alexh as she screamed, "No!"

"Back off you old fool!" Papa yelled out as he came running into the clearing.

"Papa?"

Papa hugged Alexh and then held her face as he told her, "You din't think you were out of my sight did you? I'd been here sooner but the darn elemental wasn't clear on your arrival to the birch forest. I've been hearin bout your grand adventures Alexh. I am so proud of you."

Alexh squeezed Papa with all of her might. As she released him Papa immediately turned to the Ghillie Dhu king. "And as for you, you mangled bunch of weeds! I have a bone to pick wit you! You do not represent the wisdom of the forest and you'll not be jailing my daughter."

"How dare you, Odimar! I live and breathe the forest! I know the will of the forest. What would you know? You gnomes have abandoned this world long ago. You have abandoned the magick and the forest does not work through you. I have long protected the forest from trouble like you and your daughter."

"Trouble like me?! Papa puffed and sneezed.

"Yes you gnomes with your ridiculous allergy. Trouble like you, your daughter and the rotten pixie your daughter associates with."

As the king spoke, vines slithered in around Alexh and Papa. Before they could react they found the vines tightening around them. The king signaled to the other Gillie Dhu and a large bamboo cage was dropped onto the two of them. Then the Gillie Dhu king blew onto the vines causing them to loosen and back away from the gnomes."

"Not even safe from yourselves, crazy gnomes." The king shook his head and signaled to have the bamboo cage dragged next to the iron cage. Roots suddenly came up from the ground and wound themselves around the base creating a secure jail for the two gnomes. "We shall see how to protect the forest from your sneezes gnomes." As he again shook his head and wandered away from the clearing.

Alexh looked to her Papa with watering eyes, "So, you still sneeze?"

"Sneezes? Oh no. This, this is nothing." He said as he nodded his head and looked at the situation with a sarcastic smile. "You will find that if you remember the humor in situations and stay in good spirits most of the time, the sneezes are not so bad. It gets better." He smiled again as if he was really trying to convince himself.

"So you have a plan to get out of here Papa?"

"One is coming. I can feel it. It would come faster if there were some food to eat." Papa said as he held his tummy.

Alexh remembered the snacks left in her bag. There was a

bit of sweetbread left, which she shared with Papa. She then pulled out the strange fruit and offered it to Papa.

"Hmf, goblin food." As he shook his head with his tongue hanging out.

Alexh stretched her arm out into the iron cage beside them, offering Minx the odd fruit. "Minx? Is this something that pixies will eat?"

Minx's eyes opened slightly, and then they opened wide when she saw the fruit that Alexh had to offer. She giggled quietly and accepted the fruit. She took a single bite and then rested again.

Alexh turned to her Papa again, asking, "Papa, were those stories true?"

"Oh Alexh, someday you'll be grown into someone that wouldn't recognize the gnome you are today."

"But Papa, how did you get better? What gets rid of the peptiflitter?"

"Where did you hear that word?"

Minx seemed to gain the strength to speak. "It's a pixie word." She smiled and repositioned herself so that she could better see them. Alexh noticed that Minx smiled with a peace she hadn't seen before.

Then, as if nothing had happened from the point the king left off, Minx recanted the story of Papa. "I wanted your Papa to continue to heal and I wanted to reward the bear. They were the best entertainment in the forest."

"You reward for entertainment?" Alexh asked.

Nature of the Forest

Minx took another bite of the fruit and continued to eat as she spoke, "Of course. I'm grateful for any entertainment I come across in the forest. I always find a way to help out the very best ones. This bear made me laugh every time she smacked her big smelly rump down on Odimar.." Minx's eyes became excited with glee as she continued, "He could barely breathe, but I could hear him yelling, "help, help, help", hahahaha!"

Papa furrowed his brow at her. "Hmf, silly pixies."

"The bear wanted to always be with Odimar. She fell so deeply in love with him. So, I turned her into a gnome. She must have been pretty hot for a gnome, because your papa took her straight home. They went back to the village together and married. She continued to teach Odimar to control his temper and they now have a lovely family."

"That's my Mamma?!"

"It is unnatural!" whispered a voice from outside the cage.

"But it is not unnatural. Nature brought them together. I only helped their love stick."

Another Gillie Dhu that had been placed as a guard had approached the cage with detest for the pixie story.
"This is the meddling you do. Always something to upset the balance of nature. The king will not like this." Then the Gillie Dhu vanished from sight.

"Papa, what does he mean? He won't hurt mama will he?"
"Oh no darling. Of course not. What's done is done. He just hasn't figured out what to do with us. The king has his own self imposed laws and none of them will allow for him to harm us. You needn't be worrying bout that."

Minx smiled at Alexh as she popped the last piece of fruit

into her mouth. "Mmm... goblin fruit. Their magick is so delicious."

"You're better now?" asked Alexh.

"Well, if better has nothing to do with being locked in this cage. I still can't get out. Nope, it's all up to you gnomie. Our only defense will be the laws of the forest. You've learned a lot of them. You've really learned them. The king can recite them but he hasn't had to put them all into action like you gnomie. You've really learned them. I can see it in you."

"But I'm just as trapped as you."

Minx glanced down at the vine moving across the ground. It had moved into the bamboo cage and began to pile up into one spot.

"Oh I doubt you'll have much trouble getting out now."

The vine soon became Vindr, who looked at Alexh sheepishly. "I'm here."

"Vindr!"

"Shhhh!" everyone collectively hushed Alexh.
"Vindr." She whispered. "You came back for me. I knew you had to come back for me." She squeezed Vindr and kissed his noggin.

Vindr slipped away and said with mild frustration, "Yeah, well can't let a girl out brave me, can I. So, I'm going to tell the roots to release and lift the cage high enough so you can crawl out. Then, I'll wrap myself around you so that we can get to my dad unseen. I'm hoping you have a plan from there."

"Oh yes, I do have a plan. You can trust me on that."

Nature of the Forest

Vindr looked at Alexh with doubt but signaled the roots to do their work. He blew on them until there was just enough room for Alexh to squeeze out. Papa and Minx watched them as they disappeared into the forest.

Alexh moved around in the pit of Vindr's belly realizing she is again trapped within vines. "I can't believe I chose to be in the middle of knotted vines." she whispered.

"I'm not knotted!" Vindr protested, "I'm gently wrapping you. You should be appreciating the space I've made for you."

"Oh yes. Appreciating." Alexh rolled her eyes.

Within moments Alexh could see the king. He was getting ready to sleep and had his feet soaking in a pot of warm water, just as the fir darrig had told her.

Vindr asked, "So what are you going to do?"

"I'm just going to let your dad learn from everything he's hoped and feared."

"How are you going to do that?"

Alexh snuck behind the king and poured the pouch of magick into the pot of water. Nothing seemed to happen at first. The king began to talk to himself, complaining about the situation with the gnomes and pixie.

"Rotten pixie, defying me, defying the forest. Never once considering the repercussions. Probably isn't even teachable! And what to do with the crazy gnome sneezing? It is a curse, I'm sure. Probably for abandoning the true world and its magick. How to fix them?"

As the king continued to complain his head began to grow.

"What is happening to my fathers' head?"

"I don't know, does it normally grow like that?"

"No! Our heads don't grow like that."

The king's head, an earthen and leafy mass, became noticeably larger as he fell backwards. The king yelled, "Help!" as he could not get up due to the weight of his growing noggin.

"What did you do?"

"I don't know."

"What do you mean you don't know? You irresponsible gnome! You can't go around playing with magick you don't understand. You gnomes shouldn't even play with magick!"

"That's not true! Everyone has magick!"

"Where did you get this magick. I know it's not yours."

"I can't say."

"It's goblin magick, isn't it! Those goblins playing tricks all the time!"

"You sound like your father!"

"Well obviously my father was right about you! You are dangerous."

The king's head continued to grow as Vindr and Alexh argued increasingly louder. His head became lodged between the trees and began to hurt. All he could do was whine and listen to Alexh arguing with his son as their voices became louder.

Vindr yelled at Alexh, "You are in opposition to my father and all of the forest!"

Alexh stepped back from Vindr. She was shocked that he would say such cruel things to her. Her eyes began to well up. "I can't be in opposition to the forest because I am part of it. The forest is big and grand. It's beyond anything we even know. Sometimes we play rough and it's only knowing is to play rough right back."

"What is that supposed to mean?"

"Just that your father is caught in the struggle. He has to let go of the need to control anything outside of himself ."

"What? My father is the king. It's his job to be in control."

The king heard Alexh's words. He stopped whining and became calm.

"King, I'm not separate from you and I'm not separate from the forest. I'm just as magickal and part of the forest as you." Alexh placed her hand on the kings giant head. Her words touched his heart and his head began to shrink.

Alexh stroked his head and calmly said, "I have all good intentions for you. I know the magick between us will be good from this point on. It is our differences that make us a unique expression of the forest and we can only create what is in our best interest from the magick of the forest."

The king's painful expression soon turned to relief. He looked into Alexh's deep blue eyes and felt her earnest wishes to see him healed. The mud and vines that formed his large noggin shifted and twisted and washed away as a more relaxed expression took over his face completely. The kings head returned to its natural size. Vindr approached Alexh and

asked, "How did you do this? Gnomes do not have this kind of magick."

The king responded in a softer crackling voice, "She healed me by reminding me of the natural laws of the forest." The king stood up and placed his hand on her head. "Alexh, when did you become so wise? You have been removed from the world of magick your entire life."

"Minx, the goblins and even my mother have all taught me the laws of the forest. I hope to one day know every type of folkie and understand them."

"Well my dear gnome, there is no more benevolent wishes than to want to understand each other. Thank you for reminding me."

"Does this mean you will let my Papa and Minx go?"

The king hesitated and stroked the leaves of his beard for a moment. "I'll be makin a deal with that pixie, but you needn't be worrying about their release. I can promise you that my dear."

CHAPTER 9

Going Home

The Gillie Dhu King greeted Minx and personally told her that she is to be released from the iron cage, but not before she promises not to steal from the Gillie Dhu in the future and to curtail her temptation to take what she wanted from other folkie throughout the forest. This included taking the young animals and folkies she so enjoyed stealing so much. This did not happen without a big argument. The final outcome had something to do with lazy pixies needing to become better creators rather than stealing. You are robbing yourself when you chose to depend on resources created by someone else rather than to create new ones imagined, designed and refined yourself.

Alexh had been with Vindr and Povh, who finally returned as promised. Vindr insisted upon teaching her about how he communicates with the plants, trees and wind. He showed off his ability to make the foliage around her appear to be speaking to her. He flailed his long arms out toward the plants in flamboyant gestures like a conductor of gnome orchestra. Then he affectionately blew his whisper upon the wind. The plants reacted as if life were blown into them granting innate animation.

Alexh understood that his magick was something for her to appreciate, even though it may not be a magick that she is meant to master. It was hard for her to even remember what it felt like to live in the other world where she did not have this grand variety of folkies to enjoy and learn from. Alexh learned so much about herself in this new environment that was both dangerous and magickal. It brought her lessons she didn't know that she needed and helped her resolve parts of herself she didn't know haunted her. This new place became a part of her that she could never forget. She finally understood that she was never separate from the forest and all

116

of its creation. She finally understood that every thought and action originating from her was in perfect alignment for what the forest has in mind for her. Its lessons change with her and help her to grow into a place of peace.

Vindr began making a large flower tickle and tease her when Papa snuck up from behind and pretended to be the voice of the flower. He whispered in a funny voice, "Ah, but my beauty pales in comparison to the sheen of your lovely long hair and the pretty gnome smile."

Alexh looked at the strange flower wondering where it picked up Papa's accent until he grabbed her from behind.

"So my smarty pants daughter has outsmarted the old Ghillie Dhu king, eh? I'll be expectin to hear a bit more outa yeh at storytime in the future." Papa bounced around pretending to be battling something invisible as he continued, "Meh brave young gnome havin it out wit the scary bein's in the faerie world!"

Vindr disappeared into the foliage as he snickered at the silly old gnome. He sent his farewell upon the wind to Alexh, "Until we meet again gnomie."

Alexh hugged her papa as she scolded him, "I wasn't having it out with anyone Papa. I love it here. I want to stay here forever!"

Papa took her hand and walked with her as he told her, "Alexh meh dear, this world will remain in yer heart. You will never be separated from yer path of wisdom. I know yeh love it here. But it's time to put lessons into action. Nothing is truly learnt until you put it into action."

Minx suddenly appeared to add to Papa's words of wisdom. "And you gotta teach someone else what you know so

you learn it better! Sparkle magick! Every time you teach something to another it makes you better organize your thoughts and apply the lessons in new creative ways, with perceptions you may not have otherwise considered."

Alexh hugged Minx and told her, "Minx, I need you. Can't you just come with me?"

Papa interjected, "No, Minx has pixie things to do I'm sure. She'll not be able to flit around our home doing pixie things."

Minx simply winked at Alexh telling her, "I have a present for you." Minx pulled a fancy polished rock out of nowhere and folded it into Alexh's hand continuing, "It's a magickal good luck rock."

Alexh laughed, "Ha, magickal only because it will remind of you. I know where the magick is now Minx. Thank you so much. I'll carry it with me to remind me of that." As they finally came to the doorway back to their world Alexh added, "I'm going to miss you so much!"

Minx glanced at Papa and began to comfort Alexh, "Oh silly head! Don't you know that somehow you'll be back when the time is right. Our lessons appear on time. You just stop worrying about the past and about the future. You focus on being present and opening your eyes up to the lesson in front of you. The magick will be with you instantly."

"But I love to dream about my future. How will I know what I want to be and create if I haven't imagined it? Isn't dreaming okay?"

"Dreaming is okay. You first have to focus on not letting your imagination turn to worry. Then all of your teachers will be there to help present the possibilities. All action happens in the now. Stay focused and stay present. Keep an open mind

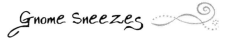

and an open heart. Respect and learn from the differences in others. And especially respect all folkies as your teachers."

"But Minx, when will I get to come back?"

Minx touched and played with Alexh's long silky hair as she responded, "Well, I promised not to steal youngsters like you anymore. I guess I'll just have to wait for you to get lost again." Minx said winking again at Alexh and giving a big grin to Papa.

Papa didn't appreciate the idea and furrowed his brow at her as he took Alexh by the arm and pulled her through the door, followed by Povh.

Upon Alexh's return to the ordinary world that is only beginning to know magick, she decided to write down a glossary of the things she learned while in the faerie world.

She needed a reminder of all of the new terms and the great lessons from her first trip. It would take some time and effort to put these lessons into action. Learning to become part of the magick is a lot of work. Learning to let go of the worry takes a lot of patience. Alexh was now learning to forgive herself and others for everything she thought before her adventure. She knew that she would still make mistakes and sometimes lose her temper. She knew that sometimes she may misunderstand others and worry too much about what they think. The most important thing to remember is that no matter what action has been taken, there will always be a teacher there waiting to be noticed.

Alexhs Glossary for
Majickal Understanding

Alexh	(a – lesh) That's me. The gnome who went on a fantastic adventure with real live goblins and gillie dhu and even a pixie. I'm the magick that I have been looking for.
Booghopper	Creature from the faerie world that jumps very high. It is grey with purple wings and expects treats when it chirps at folkies.
Bossy	Abuse of responsibility. Pushing the teacher role when it is not welcome. This inhibits lessons to self and others.
Chemistry	Pertaining to chemicals. There are millions of chemicals that move through every living thing. The more complex the plant or animal is, the more complex the chemistry. This type of chemistry can be effected by nutrients (food), environment (weather, shelter, other outside influences) or by the moods of the animal carrying these chemicals. Thought patterns trigger glands within the brain that release chemicals that trigger other reactions throughout the body, including triggering other glands with millions of other chemical possibilites.

Drowning Goblins	Pixies often push goblins into water, or otherwise trick them into getting wet. This is because goblins can't swim. Since goblins live forever like most faerie folkies, they simply take on a lot of water until they can get out. Fellow goblins must roll the waterlogged goblin until the water is all released.
Elemental	Tiny folkie that lights up like a firefly. They often play the part of messenger in the forest. They like this job because they like having the best access to all of the gossip.
Fachan	There are few good descriptions of this creature. Most who have gotten a good look died instantly from a heart attack. They are known as the ugliest creature that ever lurked in any forest. It is best not to get too close or look directly at this creature. It's purpose in the forest is to scare all living things. The only defense against him is to resist fear.
Faerie Door	A hidden vortex to another dimension where the faerie folk come from. The vortex has a slight pull that gnomes cannot feel. A tree growing nearby can feel this doorway and gets pulled around the doorway until it creates an archway. This is handy for finding the vortexes.

Fir Darrig	A very old and mischievous creature who uses tricks to do what he believes is in the best interest of others. He likes to make bargains.
Geode	A lumpy round rock that is full of crystal. Pixies can use them for illusion magick.
Gillie Dhu	Folkies that support the natural energies of the forest. They look and act like the forest itself.
Hormone	Wonky stuff that runs through my body. It is produced by the brain and various glands in the body and causes changes. Some changes are long lasting and some are temporary. Some changes happen very quickly and some take a long time. Hormones can change the way you feel, the way you look and how your body works. Some hormones, like with the caterpillar, can cause a body to completely deteriorate, while a new body forms from the sludge. A body can be capable of producing thousands of hormones at once that are proteins, peptides, modified amino acids or steroids.
Implantaion	Gestation in an animal has been temporarily suspended by the emotional expression effecting the hormonal output.
Infinite	There is no end. The knowledge of the forest and the extent of possibilities of creation through the forest best demonstrates this word.

Iron Poisoning	A sickness that etheric faerie folkie get when exposed to iron. It will cause them to snap back into the faerie dimension for healing from this allergy.
Life Force, The	Etheric Folkies like Pixies call the life force that runs through all things and each other the Magick. Gnomes honor the forest as this life force. Some other faerie folkie believe it originates from the heart of any creature and others believe it comes from the first faeries. Others believe that all faerie folkie are correct and there is no one source.
Magick	Magick is a broad term that is defined differently by all folkies. Pixies and other etheric faerie folkie call the life force that runs through all things Magick. Gnomes refer to their special talents as their magick. All living beings have a relationship with Magick and use it differently in their lives. Magick can also be described as a special coincidence or a special relationship.
Ogre	1. A large crabby folkie that believes he is grander than all others. 2.Ego, arrogance 3. The most important part of self to learn from
Patagium	Thin layer of skin that runs along the side of gliding animal as an extension of the abdomen, connecting the limbs. It works similar to wings for bats, sugar gliders and some squirrels and lizards.

Peptiflitter   The condition of being overwhelmed by frustration or anger. The body is flooded by pepti's, which are chemicals that the body produces. The body gets used to always working with the same chemicals. It is a lot of work to make a body change the type of chemicals it is used to. The only way to do this is to become very aware of your mood at all times and learn to refocus whenever necessary.

Predator   A creature that hunts another creature.

Responsibility   Accountability to self rather than to others. You have responsibility to manage yourself in a way that is conducive to becoming more creative and knowledgeable every day. You have a responsibility to your own happiness and to no one else's. No one has responsibility to your happiness. You are responsible to playing the teacher role in another's experience, only when they ask for your assistance and never when your role as a teacher is not welcome.

Student   A part of everyone that welcomes knowledge.

Sugar glider	A small marsupial that can glide short distances between trees. Some gnome parents find the largest sugar gliders for riding. Because glider communities are mostly made up of female gliders, males must go out on their own. Of these lone gliders, the best are chosen for bonding with a young gnome. The gliders generally prefer to be awake at night, but when they find that the force of gravity is changed slightly while carrying their gnome, they spend more time awake during the day. Gliders who carry gnomes are gravitized to trees rather than the ground, making them glide further than gliders who are not carrying gnomes. They still sleep a lot between riding and are often given the job of night watch. A glider will bond to one rider for life and remain very loyal.
Teacher	A part of everyone that possesses wisdom and understanding. This is a role that is taken when the sharing of wisdom is welcomed by another.
Ticklebird	Another odd creature observed in the faerie world. It is a bird that cannot fly. It has long dangly feathers on its wings, which are used to tickle unsuspecting folkies into submission. Then they take the folkies snacks and run away.

Alexhs Glossary

Trows   Troll like creature that is small and nibble. They generally play tricks on other folkie as well as animals. They live in trees and have fantastic appetites and are the best dancers in the forest.

Learn more at http://www.gnomesneezes.com